the fire of REVIVAL

by
Ryan LeStrange

Published by Harrison House LLC
Tulsa, OK

Unless otherwise marked, scripture quotations are from the *King James Version* of the Bible.

14 13 12 11   10 9 8 7 6 5 4 3 2 1

The Fire of Revival
ISBN: 978-1-60683-410-7

Copyright ©2011 by Ryan LeStrange
P.O. Box 16206
Bristol, VA 24209

Published by Harrison House, Inc.
P.O. Box 35035
Tulsa, OK 74153
www.HarrisonHouse.com

CONTENTS

ENDORSEMENTS

Ryan LeStrange is a young minister that came to my Bible College in Cleveland, TN. After he graduated, he stayed over for several years to help us at the ministry. Then he left to help another ministry up in Virginia. After that he went to Bristol, VA and started a church.

It wasn't very long until he had it full of people. The reason he did is because he is called of God and has a gift of God to preach and to teach. He has the gifts of the Holy Spirit inside of him and they operate through him. The word of wisdom, word of knowledge, discerning of spirits, the gifts of healings, working of miracles, faith, prophecy, tongues and interpretation all operate through him. They do because he learned in Bible College that if you want to have a New Testament church then you need to have these things operating in your ministry. And he yielded himself to God and so now he has a good, strong, faithful church.

I love Ryan and you can trust him. You can trust him to come to your church. You can trust him to go speak for you because he's a real, strong, young man of God that is totally honest and I have found him to be one of God's chosen vessels.

Dr. Norvel Hayes

I first got to know Ryan in 1993 when he came to New Life Bible College. He had come from California and had a desire to be in television. He was young, smart and driven. God got a hold of him though and he spent the next two years seeking after God. He didn't work a job or spend all of his time hanging out with friends. He would come to school and then go home and get on his face before God.

After he graduated, the Lord showed me to make him the administrator of the Bible College and an associate pastor at the church. He became part of the team that would travel with me when I ministered around the country. He worked for my dad and me for several years before God sent him out to start his own ministry. Now he is well established in his own ministry and is planting churches and spreading the Gospel all over the world with signs and wonders following.

Today Ryan is a close personal friend of mine. I have seen his life and ministry and know him to be a man of great honor, character and integrity. He preaches truth and is not one to "tickle the ears" of the listener. He is an anointed minister, a great husband and father and one who seeks the face of God. He has a vision to see the world saved, a drive to get it done and the determination to see it through. I know that you will be blessed and ministered to by reading this book!

Zona Hayes-Morrow

INTRODUCTION

Wilt thou not revive us again:
that thy people may rejoice in thee?
Psalm 85:6

I was preparing to do what I love to do, preach the Word of God in a local church. This was not just any church but one that was led by a very dear friend. This particular church holds a lot of special memories for me. It is a place that God used to ignite a fire in my life that has never died.

As I was in prayer preparing my heart for the time of ministry, the Holy Spirit quickened something powerful in my spirit. He told me to get ready, that the service I was about to go into would not be just the start of another series of meetings but a move of God. When the Lord spoke this to me, my mind began to race. I wondered what would happen. How would it happen? What did I need to do to prepare? All of these were questions to which I would not receive an answer. It is amazing how the carnal mind has difficulty flowing with the things of the Spirit. When you truly learn to live in the Spirit you subdue your natural mind.

The natural mind will attempt to throw you off course but radical obedience comes from the spirit realm.

When I arrived at the church where I was to preach, I was immediately met with an uncommon sense of passion and hunger in the hearts of the people. I could tangibly feel the electrified presence of God in the building. The glory of the Lord was overwhelming at times.

It was evident from the first moment of that initial service that this was no ordinary meeting. It was something far deeper. It was something quite uncommon: an awakening! Throughout the several days of meetings, God's fire manifested, melting yokes and bondages off the lives of those in attendance. Hungry people came and filled every seat in the building. Bodies were healed as God poured out amazing miracles. Some of the hardest hearts were turned toward the Lord.

As I walked to my car after the meetings, people would greet me and tell me how they had come back to the Lord. One young man had such an encounter with God that he decided to walk away from a life of addiction and bondage to serve Him. People who had become hardened and cold toward the things of God were suddenly tender and knelt at the altar weeping. I was ecstatic!

Every day God revealed Himself in new and different ways during these glorious meetings. It reminded me of many years earlier when I had first begun in ministry. The Holy Spirit would show up and do such marvelous things that the natural mind could not figure it out. Suddenly, there was a heightened awareness in my spirit of the glory of God. Something deep was happening in the spirit realm. My mind wondered what was happening, what was this? God what are you doing? I want to be in tune with you. The answer would come shortly.

After such a powerful presence with God, it was time to leave the meetings to return home and preach at my church on Sunday. I called a good minister friend of mine to report the wondrous things that God had done. She asked me how I could describe what had happened. I told her that it could only be described fully with one word: revival. God's people were being revived, awakened, and refreshed in order to prepare us for the harvest that is soon coming.

My minister friend asked me if I thought that this was just something happening in this particular series of meetings or if we were in a season of revival. At that moment I did not know the answer to that question. When I arrived home, I decided to go into prayer for our church services which would be held the next day, Sunday. It was in this time of prayer that God told me with certainty that He was going to visit our church with the same power, the same atmosphere as the revival we had just experienced. God instructed me to call for special Friday and Saturday night revival services. Again, my natural mind struggled with the Word of the Lord. I wondered how we would have special meetings with no guest speaker. Would people come? What would happen? Was I really hearing from heaven or was I basking in the afterglow of the refreshing revival move I had just experienced?

I hid the Word of the Lord in my heart and decided that I would see what happened in the service the next morning. That morning, during the praise and worship portion of our service, the power of God fell like electrified fire. You could feel the burning presence of the Lord in an overwhelming way. The same revival presence that had overtaken me in my travels was there in our home church! I knew at that moment that I had indeed heard from the Lord the night before and that this was a significant moment not just for a church but for the Body of Christ. Revival fire was hitting the land.

Our church began having revival meetings on Friday and Saturday nights. We had little advertisement, no guest speaker and no frills. Still, we had one thing in abundance, the radical presence of God with signs and wonders. Hungry people came from all over our region and God sparked a regional fire. What no man could do, God did in a moment.

God's power gripped every part of my being, igniting a passion that consumed me. Many people came to me to report the same type of consuming encounter with God. They found it difficult to think about natural things because their minds were filled with God thoughts. It was like a wave that swept every willing person up in the flow. Everything changed. The way we did church changed. The way we did worship in those meetings changed. Our priorities and plans changed. We had encountered something that altered our entire sate of being. We had been consumed by **The Fire of Revival.**

1

WHAT IS REVIVAL?

I t is impossible to walk in anything that you do not understand. The first and most fundamental question that many people have is: What is revival? This question sparks debate, discussion, and holds many possible answers.

First, let's begin with a simple definition. Revival simply means to bring back to life. You are not dealing with something or someone that has no life but rather something or someone that was once full of life but has somehow lost much of that life. It is the breathing in of fresh life and wind.

Revival is a wave that overtakes churches, cities, and regions with the power of God. When revival rushes into a community it turns things upside down and ushers hearts back into the deeper things of God. Revival is a city-shaking movement. All historical revivals spilled out of the four walls of any church or meeting and extended into cities and then regions and nations.

Repent ye therefore, and be converted, that your sins may be blotted out, when the times of refreshing shall come from the presence of the Lord.

Acts 3:19

Repentance is at the forefront of revival. People begin to be more God-conscious which drives them to the Lord asking for forgiveness. As they draw near to Him, times of refreshing flow from heaven.

When revival comes alive in the hearts of God's people they begin to humble themselves before the Lord. It is not a religious humility but a heartfelt expression of gratitude and a desire to please the King of Kings.

For thus saith the high and lofty One that inhabiteth eternity, whose name is Holy; I dwell in the high and holy place, with him also that is of a contrite and humble spirit, to revive the spirit of the humble, and to revive the heart of the contrite ones.

Isaiah 57:15

Oh that thou wouldest rend the heavens, that thou wouldest come down, that the mountains might flow down at thy presence, As when the melting fire burneth, the fire causeth the waters to boil, to make thy name known to thine adversaries, that the nations may tremble at thy presence! When thou didst terrible things which we looked not for, thou camest down, the mountains flowed down at thy presence.

Isaiah 64:1-3

Revival is a time in which God comes in His fullness. Impossible miracles take place in the midst of true revival. The most broken people are restored in the fire of revival. Revival is the absolute manifestation of the presence of God Almighty in the midst of His people.

Revival brings an awakening to the Church. When revival fire begins to burn it brings a new sense of urgency for the things of God. In a moment, people are awakened to their destiny which previously remained hidden as the devil had blinded their eyes.

Because thou sayest, I am rich, and increased with goods, and have need of nothing; and knowest not that thou art wretched, and miserable, and poor, and blind, and naked: I counsel thee to buy of me gold tried in the fire, that thou mayest be rich; and white raiment, that thou mayest be clothed, and that the shame of thy nakedness do not appear; and anoint thine eyes with eyesalve, that thou mayest see.

Revelation 3:17-18

The church of Laodicea had drifted away from their first love. They had become ensnared in prosperity, comfort, and easy living, much like the American Church in this day. They were preaching, having services, and living life as normal yet they had grown cold in their hearts.

It is amazingly easy for people to start out serving God with humility and hunger, then end up blinded by complacency. This is what had happened to the Laodicean church. Their eyes were blinded to the deeper things of God.

Jesus told the Laodecian church to repent and return to their first love. Revival is always a move of repentance. As the revival fire of God falls upon churches and communities, people will return to their first love. In that process of return there is a great deliverance that takes place. God's people are delivered from distraction, deception, and the lies of the enemy as their hearts are purified by holy fire.

Jesus instructed the Laodicean church to anoint their eyes with eye salve. I believe that this is a clear instruction to get the prophetic vision and ministry restored to the House of God.

> *Surely the Lord GOD will do nothing, but he revealeth his secret unto his servants the prophets.*
>
> *Amos 3:7*

In the Old Testament, God referred to the prophets as seers. They were anointed by the Lord to receive vital instruction for the people of God. Their entire ministry was based on revelation knowledge and calling the people of God forth into their ministries and out of bondage.

The Church is blinded when the prophetic ministry is cut off. It is the prophetic ministry that brings forth the fire of repentance and calls people to return to their first love. It is also the prophetic ministry that provides crucial instruction and direction for the Body of Christ. How is it that the Church can become so disconnected from the heart of God?

I spoke recently with a friend who attends a large church that is in the seeker-friendly movement. She explained to me that her Pastor had modeled their church after the ministry of Jesus. She went on to say that just as Jesus had drawn large crowds and then discipled a portion of those crowds, this was also the mission of their church. In order for these churches to draw a large crowd they make sure that the worship is not too spiritual so that it will not offend the unbeliever. They have no altar calls or corporate calls to salvation as this might be offensive to the unbeliever. Every sermon is carefully critiqued and planned to make sure that nothing will challenge those in attendance as this might diminish the crowd. Still, somehow they compare this to the ministry of Jesus.

Are they reading the same Bible that I read? Jesus' ministry was bold, marked and confirmed by the power of God. Jesus did not water down the gospel to attract a crowd. In fact, the more radical that Jesus was, the bigger the crowds. They came to experience the miracles, deliverances, and power of God in His ministry.

And at even, when the sun did set, they brought unto him all that were diseased, and them that were possessed with devils. And all the city was gathered together at the door. And he healed many that were sick of divers diseases, and cast out many devils; and suffered not the devils to speak, because they knew him.

Mark 1:32-34

I can find no place in Scripture where Jesus changed what He believed to satisfy people. There is no nice, seeker-friendly, nonconfrontational way to cast the devil out of someone. Revival fire is calling the Church back to the raw power of God. We must turn away from the socially popular, humanistic philosophy that is trying to overthrow legitimate gospel ministry. How can we as a people return to the ministry of Jesus? One major component is through the prophetic anointing.

God is raising up a prophetic people who are thirsty to hear from heaven. The Prophets shall stand and declare the mark of destiny for this hour. The revival fire must overthrow the anti-revival methodology of church. We must realize that there are churches in the land that are propagating a powerless gospel that is choking out the vital ministry of Jesus. Spirit-filled believers are giving their time and money to these churches because they are comfortable and convenient. In the meantime, the moral compass of our nation is drifting tragically off course. These churches provide a model of ministry that is seducing young Pastors away from the move of God and empowering a spirit of religion to rule cities. Just as the Laodicean church took comfort in its financial and numerical success, so too these ministries gauge their impact by counting people and money, yet they are void of the presence of God.

Quench not the Spirit. Despise not prophesyings.

1 Thessalonians 5:19-20

The types of churches that I have mentioned above have virtually no understanding of the ministry of the Holy Spirit. In Acts chapter two, the very first meeting of the Early Church was a revival meeting filled with radical displays of a move of the Spirit. We can not afford to quench the work of the Spirit in the Church of this hour. We must not despise the gift of prophecy. In fact, the Church should seek God for manifestations of the gift of prophecy.

Wherefore, brethren, covet to prophesy, and forbid not to speak with tongues.

1 Corinthians 14:39

The prophetic ministry is a vital part of God's end-time plan for His people. It is the Prophets who will prophesy God's plans and purposes in these last days. We need the fire that comes in the presence of the prophetic anointing.

Ho, every one that thirsteth, come ye to the waters, and he that hath no money; come ye, buy, and eat; yea, come, buy wine and milk without money and without price. Wherefore do ye spend money for that which is not bread? and your labour for that which satisfieth not? hearken diligently unto me, and eat ye that which is good, and let your soul delight itself in fatness. Incline your ear, and come unto me: hear, and your soul shall live; and I will make an everlasting covenant with you, even the sure mercies of David.

Isaiah 55:1-3

How does revival come? It comes when men and women get desperate for God. Revival begins with spiritual hunger, when God's people are no longer satisfied with man's plan but they long for something more. Jesus told all hungry people to come to Him. He is attracted to hunger.

Blessed are they which do hunger and thirst after righteousness: for they shall be filled.

Matthew 5:6

There are many people who are not hungry to go any deeper. They like having God in a box. They want just enough of Him to feel better and possibly be blessed but they do not long for a deeper walk. God cannot fill those people in the manner that He desires. His promise is to fill the hungry. He is placing a divine hunger on the inside of men and women who will begin to seek

Him for something deeper than what they are walking in right now. That is revival hunger!

Jesus encountered a broken woman standing at the well one day. She had been through the pain of multiple divorces and was living in sin. She probably felt broken and ashamed. It seemed as though there was no hope for her. I am sure that she condemned herself and believed that she could never do anything valuable for God.

Jesus answered and said unto her, Whosoever drinketh of this water shall thirst again: But whosoever drinketh of the water that I shall give him shall never thirst; but the water that I shall give him shall be in him a well of water springing up into everlasting life. The woman saith unto him, Sir, give me this water, that I thirst not, neither come hither to draw. Jesus saith unto her, Go, call thy husband, and come hither. The woman answered and said, I have no husband. Jesus said unto her, Thou hast well said, I have no husband: For thou hast had five husbands; and he whom thou now hast is not thy husband: in that saidst thou truly. The woman saith unto him, Sir, I perceive that thou art a prophet.

John 4:13-19

Many people are like this woman. They are ashamed of their past and feel as though all hope has left them. They have no real sense of purpose or spiritual identity. God has a plan for every person. He longs to pour His living water into their wounds just like He did that woman.

He desires to do the same thing today in the lives of the hurting. His power is available to set them free. Revival is an atmosphere of healing and freedom for the hurting.

> *The woman then left her waterpot, and went her way into the city, and saith to the men, Come, see a man, which told me all things that ever I did: is not this the Christ? Then they went out of the city, and came unto him.*
>
> *John 4:28-30*

This woman was transformed by the ministry of Jesus. She left His presence and told her entire city about Him. She was the first woman Evangelist in the New Testament. One encounter with the living Christ changed her forever. This is the mighty work that God desires to do in the move of revival. A broken generation will find freedom and purpose in His presence.

There is a reason that you are reading this book. God has placed a seed of revival in your spirit. He is positioning you in hunger so you will draw upon Him for living water. The living water will heal you and bring you into your destiny.

Revival is beckoning. The flames are calling out to a generation to rise higher and go deeper. Revival is being sent to unlock hidden purpose and undying passion.

2

THE HEADSHIP
OF JESUS

And hath put all things under his feet, and gave him to be
the head over all things to the church, which is his body, the
fulness of him that filleth all in all.
Ephesians 1:22-23

Jesus holds the unique position as the Head of the New Testament Church. The Church is His Body manifest in the earth. This means that the primary assignment of the Church is to manifest the love, power, authority, and Kingdom of God in the earth. This is a sacred task committed to the saints of God. We have been supernaturally endued with power from on high so we can get the job done.

One of the definitions that we have given for revival is: *a city-shaking movement, a wave that overtakes cities with the power of God.* Jesus was a Revivalist. His ministry did not just impact individuals, which is a valuable ministry, His ministry affected entire cities.

And whithersoever he entered, into villages, or cities, or country, they laid the sick in the streets, and besought him that they might touch if it were but the border of his garment: and as many as touched him were made whole.

Mark 6:56

How God anointed Jesus of Nazareth with the Holy Ghost and with power: who went about doing good, and healing all that were oppressed of the devil; for God was with him.

Acts 10:38

The power of God upon the life and ministry of Jesus was so strong that everywhere He went there was divine change. This change caused cities to be shaken with the glory of God.

And he came to Nazareth, where he had been brought up: and, as his custom was, he went into the synagogue on the sabbath day, and stood up for to read And there was delivered unto him the book of the prophet Esaias. And when he had opened the book, he found the place where it was written, The Spirit of the Lord is upon me, because he hath anointed me to preach the gospel to the poor; he hath sent me to heal the brokenhearted, to preach deliverance to the captives, and recovering of sight to the blind, to set at liberty them that are bruised, To preach the acceptable year of the Lord. And he closed the book, and he gave it again to the minister, and sat down. And the eyes of all them that were in the synagogue were fastened on him. And he began to say unto them, This day is this scripture fulfilled in your ears.

Luke 4:16–21

Jesus was launching His public ministry as He read this text. He was proclaiming the anointing that God had placed upon His life to embark on the most powerful three and a half years in history. In these verses there are powerful clues to the revival anointing that we must examine.

All five ministry gifts are covered in these profound statements about the ministry of Jesus:

1. *Preach the gospel to the poor: <u>teaching ministry</u>. The ministry of teaching delivers people from spiritual, emotional, and financial poverty as they are taught how to walk in victory.*

2. *Heal the brokenhearted: <u>pastoral ministry</u>. The pastoral anointing brings healing to even the deepest wounds as the love of the Father flows from the pastoral office.*

3. *Deliverance to the captive: <u>evangelistic ministry</u>. The evangelistic ministry releases people from the struggle of sin and condemnation as they come into the knowledge of what took place at Calvary.*

4. *Recovering of sight to the blind: <u>prophetic ministry</u>. As we discussed earlier the prophetic ministry releases spiritual vision and insight.*

5. *Set at liberty them that are bruised: <u>apostolic ministry</u>. The apostolic ministry is a radical pioneering gift that is sent to particular people and regions. The apostolic anointing confronts the spiritual rulers and provides a dynamic breakthrough.*

Jesus revealed Himself in this text. He personally carried all five ministry gifts inside of His ministry. That is why He could go into a territory and spark a sweeping revival that would minister to the hungry and anger the religious. As the Head of the Church, Jesus flowed in all five ministry graces because He is our ultimate example.

Let's examine the five-fold ministry as revealed in another text along with two other vital gifts to the Body:

And God hath set some in the church, first apostles, secondarily prophets, thirdly teachers, after that miracles, then gifts of healings, helps, governments, diversities of tongues.

1 Corinthians 12:28

1. **Apostles** - *builders, spiritual generals, multi-taskers, sent-ones, spiritual fathers, revivalists. This office is at the forefront of the move of God. They build, lead, and govern ministries and spiritual movements.*

2. **Prophets** - *seers, revealers, God-seekers, truth-tellers. Prophets are sent to guide the Body and make the heart of God known. They are called to live in the realm of the Spirit. They are God-seekers in this generation.*

3. **Teachers** - *explainers, instructors, line upon line builders of revelation. Teachers are called to bring balance to the Body of Christ by establishing fundamental doctrine. This gift is imperative for the last-day move of God. They keep the Church rooted in the Word.*

4. **Miracles (Evangelists)** - *fire starters, miracle ministers, good news reporters. The Evangelist must have the working of miracles in the forefront of their ministry. Miracles back up their proclamation of the good news!*

5. **Healings (Pastors)** - *lovers of people (sheep), instruments of healing, discipleship leaders, and leaders of local churches. Pastors are called to express the love of God to people. They bring healing to the deepest wounds as they cement people into the ministry of the local church. They are sheep minded.*

6. **Helps** - *this is a key gift in the last days revival. There are two realms of helps ministries–*

   Financial Helps - *These are gospel entrepreneurs. They go out into the world and bring finances into the Kingdom of God. They are called to finance the end-time harvest. They are anointed to be business Apostles and Prophets. They do business supernaturally and their businesses are the Lord's storehouses.*

   Service Helps - *This is the gift of serving the Body of Christ through natural acts of love and kindness. This gift is needed to fulfill the plans of the five-fold ministry gifts. Without an anointed ministry of helps team, the five-fold leaders will grow weary.*

7. **Governments** - *This is an administrative gift. The gift of governments is a more natural version of the Apostle. They take the vision of the five-fold gifts and create structured plans to fulfill that vision. They organize and lead the helps teams.*

> *And he gave some, apostles; and some, prophets; and some, evangelists; and some, pastors and teachers; For the perfecting of the saints, for the work of the ministry, for the edifying of the body of Christ.*
>
> *Ephesians 4:11-12*

God provided these unique giftings to bring the Body of Christ to the place of maturity and spiritual power. In Luke 4:19, Jesus said the result of these five ministries was to preach the acceptable year of the Lord. That is Jubilee, a time of supernatural freedom and power. As these seven dimensions of God are manifested in His Body there is release of overwhelming glory and strength.

We must ask, what is the revival anointing? The revival anointing is the culmination and cooperation of all five ministry gifts: *apostolic, prophetic, pastoral, teaching, and evangelistic, plus the two service gifts of helps and governments.* The revival that is upon us in this hour incorporates all of these cleansing streams. The Church can not pick and choose which gifts we will honor and which we will not. It takes all of the gifts to get the job done.

The five-fold ministry leaders must be delivered from a prideful spirit and come together in humility to serve the Body of Christ. In order to properly equip the Church and manifest the city-shaking revival anointing, all five gifts must work together. Each gift carries a particular anointing or empowerment.

> *And it shall come to pass in that day, that his burden shall be taken away from off thy shoulder, and his yoke from off thy neck, and the yoke shall be destroyed because of the anointing.*
>
> *Isaiah 10:27*

The anointing will destroy certain yokes in its own unique way but when all five streams come together, there is a revival river that is capable of destroying every yoke!

3

REVIVAL SPARKS

The fire of revival is much like a natural fire in that it takes a spark to begin the flame. Prayer and intercession are two of the vital sparks needed to ignite the fire of revival in various cities and regions. I meet powerful intercessors often as I travel to minister and they are unique people who develop such an intense walk with God that moments in their presence ignite a passion in your spirit.

Many of these men and women have been through mighty spiritual battles and have stood strong. They have often stood alone crying out for a church, a city, or a region. Intercessors have hearts that burn with endless passion for the move of God. While others are satisfied with church as usual, these mighty men and women wrestle with a holy dissatisfaction. They are not pleased until the presence of God comes forth in their churches.

I see a tidal wave of prophetic intercession coming. Over the past several years many prayer movements have been birthed employing worship as a key battle weapon. Only God could have planned something so unique. Many seasoned intercessors find no need for live worship music while praying but this younger generation has found a David anointing and has taken its place of battle in the army.

This move of intercession and revival will be cross-generational. We have to incorporate every age. God has commissioned prayer warriors who will boldly walk the floor reminding God of His Word and praying heaven down to earth. He has also raised up young men and women armed with prophetic music who are igniting a whole new generation of prayer warriors.

Peter therefore was kept in prison: but prayer was made without ceasing of the church unto God for him. And when Herod would have brought him forth, the same night Peter was sleeping between two soldiers, bound with two chains: and the keepers before the door kept the prison. And, behold, the angel of the Lord came upon him, and a light shined in the prison: and he smote Peter on the side, and raised him up, saying, Arise up quickly. And his chains fell off from his hands. And the angel said unto him, Gird thyself, and bind on thy sandals. And so he did. And he saith unto him, Cast thy garment about thee, and follow me. And he went out, and followed him; and wist not that it was true which was done by the angel; but thought he saw a vision. When they were past the first and the second ward, they came unto the iron gate that leadeth unto the city; which opened to them of his own accord: and they went out, and passed on through one street; and forthwith the angel departed from him. And when

Peter was come to himself, he said, Now I know of a surety, that the
LORD hath sent his angel, and hath delivered me out of the hand
of Herod, and from all the expectation of the people of the Jews. And
when he had considered the thing, he came to the house of Mary the
mother of John, whose surname was Mark; where many were gath-
ered together praying.

Acts 12:5-12

The unrelenting prayer of the Church turned away a demonic assignment that had arisen against Peter. What if the Early
Church had not yielded to prayer and intercession? They would
have allowed the devil to destroy the ministry of their spiritual
father and the plan of God would have been severely impeded.

We must have dedicated intercessors who turn back the plans
of the enemy. The devil is not going to let us move into the fire of
revival without challenging us. God has already given us victory
over the devil and delegated His power and authority to us. It is
our job as believers to manifest that authority through faith.

Then he called his twelve disciples together, and gave them power and
authority over all devils, and to cure diseases.

Luke 9:1

One way that we manifest that authority is in prayer. The
Church holds the power to bind evil spiritual forces over our cities
and loose the glory of God.

Their heart cried unto the LORD, O wall of the daughter of Zion, let
tears run down like a river day and night: give thyself no rest; let not
the apple of thine eye cease. Arise, cry out in the night: in the begin-

31

> *ning of the watches pour out thine heart like water before the face of*
> *the LORD: lift up thy hands toward him for the life of thy young*
> *children, that faint for hunger in the top of every street.*
>
> *Lamentations 2:18-19*

Those who are called to spark the fire of revival through intercession will begin to burn with a desire to pray for their assigned place. God is releasing the spirit of intercession upon His Bride. In these final moments of the Church age there is a drawing into the inner chambers of the House of God Almighty. We are being beckoned by the great Creator of all things to arise and cry out to heaven.

One of the great tools of the devil is to make intercessors feel insignificant. The enemy will tell prayer warriors that what they are doing is of none effect but that is a lie from hell. Mighty intercession in the Spirit is one of the key sparks to this last-day revival. Every Revivalist, Pastor, Apostle, or ministry leader of any kind must recognize the need for intercession. We must begin to call forth the intercessors and cast a vision for prayer warriors to arise. Then we must find leaders who are committed to prayer and have them organize prayer ministries.

No two prayer ministries will be just alike. Relationship with Jesus is extremely personal and intimate. It is foolish of us to think that everyone's relationship with the Lover of Their Soul will be just like ours. Prayer and worship are multi-faceted and unique. While there is such individuality in prayer, there are some keys that every prayer warrior can apply. Let's examine some of these keys while keeping in mind that your particular expression of prayer will be individual.

Revival is about shaking a church, city, and region. It is another realm of prayer. God is birthing a cry for lands in the realm of the spirit. He is raising up people to intercede for a move of His Spirit in the land. The primary knowledge that an intercessor must have concerning governing prayer is found in Matthew 16:19 - prayer that rules territories.

And I will give unto thee the keys of the kingdom of heaven: and whatsoever thou shalt bind on earth shall be bound in heaven: and whatsoever thou shalt loose on earth shall be loosed in heaven.

Matthew 16:19

These are patterns of prevailing prayer. Your prayer will become more effective by utilizing these power principles.

1. ***All authority has BEEN given*** - in order to pray effectively, a believer must have revelation of the complete work of Calvary. Jesus had all authority and He gave His authority to the Church!

And Jesus came and spake unto them, saying, All power is given unto me in heaven and in earth. Go ye therefore, and teach all nations, baptizing them in the name of the Father, and of the Son, and of the Holy Ghost.

Matthew 28:18-19

And what is the exceeding greatness of his power to us-ward who believe, according to the working of his mighty power, Which he wrought in Christ, when he raised him from the dead, and set him at his own right hand in the heavenly places, Far above all princi-

pality, and power, and might, and dominion, and every name that is named, not only in this world, but also in that which is to come: And hath put all things under his feet, and gave him to be the head over all things to the church, Which is his body, the fulness of him that filleth all in all.

Ephesians 1:19-23

Jesus defeated the devil. He stripped him of the authority that Adam had given him by his transgression. Jesus was the second Adam, the second God-man. He lived without sin and took upon Him our sin at the cross. Today the Body of Christ is commissioned to be the full manifestation of Jesus in this earth. We have been granted His power and authority.

As we go into intercessory prayer we are not trying to gain the authority of Christ, we already have it. We are exercising dominion by claiming the Word of God over our church, family, leaders, city, and nation. Worship is another tool in the intercessor's tool belt. Praise and worship stop the work of hell. Spirit-led, Word-based prayer, mixed with worship, is the mark of victory!

2. **God can only answer faith-filled prayers.** It takes faith to please God. Heaven responds to prayers of faith! Intercessors must prophesy (speak the revealed Word of the Lord) to situations.

> *But without faith it is impossible to please him : for he that cometh to God must believe that he is, and that he is a rewarder of them that diligently seek him.*

Hebrews 11:6

Thou shalt also decree a thing, and it shall be established unto thee:
and the light shall shine upon thy ways.

Job 22:28

God is raising up intercessors who will not listen to what the
devil says about their church or city. He wants His people to rise
up by faith and decree the Word of God. It is key that the intercessor has a solid Word base upon which to build. The Word of God
is the ultimate weapon in prayer. We are to speak just as Jesus did
to the fig tree (Mark 11:23).

And I sought for a man among them, that should make up the hedge,
and stand in the gap before me for the land, that I should not destroy
it: but I found none.

Ezekiel 22:30

The Lord is looking for people who will rise up and take hold
of His promises over cities, churches, and people. This is a holy
assignment. As intercessors begin to take their positions in the
spirit, they build a hedge of protection in prayer.

Intercessors will experience many different realms in prayer:

1. ***Prayers of faith.*** *This is the realm in which you are simply*
   standing in agreement with the Word. This is a powerful
   realm of prayer because it is based solely on what God said,
   apart from all human thought or emotion.

2. ***Deep groanings.*** *This is a realm of supernatural interces-*
   sion when the Holy Ghost takes control and sounds begin
   to burst forth from your belly so deep you can hardly bear
   up under it. This is an urgent prayer that comes and goes in

a moment's notice. *The result of this type of prayer is usually a miraculous breakthrough.*

3. **Prophetic praying.** *This is a type of prayer in which there is a unique partnership with the Holy Ghost. As you pray in tongues, the Holy Spirit begins to provide interpretations and you decree things in your known language. You find yourself praying for things and areas that you never imagined. God created everything in the known world by words and has endued us with that same creative faith. In this realm of prayer, your mouth is employed as the prophetic mouthpiece of the Lord.*

4. **Prayers of agreement.** *I have been to many prayer meetings where the people were praying over requests and screaming so loud that nobody even knew what was being prayed. It is critical in the prayer of agreement that each party involved understands exactly what the request is and releases their faith on that request. Once faith has been released, a covenant of agreement is formed. In order for this type of prayer to be effective the parties involved must stand and not move off the promise.*

5. **Worship.** *In the Old Testament, God often instructed Israel to go into worship before the battle. Worship is a key tool to release victory and shut the mouth of the devil. Minstrels also unlock the prophetic gifting, inspiring intense worship that will bring you into a realm where you more effectively hear from God.*

6. **_Praying in the Spirit._** *We will cover this in greater detail later but personal prayer in the Spirit is a must for every prayer warrior. It is imperative that an intercessor has an active prayer life in the Holy Ghost. This will build a deep foundation upon which the intercessory prayer ministry can be built.*

4

THE RIVERS OF REVIVAL

And Isaac digged again the wells of water, which they had
digged in the days of Abraham his father;
for the Philistines had stopped them after the death of
Abraham: and he called their names after the names by which
his father had called them. And Isaac's servants digged in the
valley, and found there a well of springing water.
Genesis 26:18-19

Isaac began to dig the wells that had been stopped up. The wells were filled with earth. Man was formed from the dust of the earth. When man places his ability and intellect above the ways of God it stops up the flow of living waters.

We are living in a revival moment. God wants to release a flow of His presence that will sweep the Church into a greater move of His Spirit. The Philistines had stopped up the wells. Philistines were people who were against God. They were a type and shadow of demonic power.

Demon spirits have been assigned against the Spirit-filled Church to hold back the move of God. Though the devil may try, he cannot stop what God is doing. There is a realm of worship that is being birthed in this hour that will send hell running!

> *Out of the mouth of babes and sucklings hast thou ordained strength because of thine enemies, that thou mightest still the enemy and the avenger.*
>
> *Psalm 8:2*

Anointed worship is a mighty tool to stop the attacks of hell. In this hour of revival, God is raising up an army of worshippers who will reclaim the wells of revival that the devil and human efforts have stopped up.

There is a new sound coming forth in the Spirit. God is releasing songs of healing, songs of salvation, songs of deliverance, and songs for battle into the spirits of anointed psalmists. The psalmists must confidently take their place and know that God has raised them up as leaders in the last-day revival that He has brought to refresh His people.

> *But the Spirit of the Lord departed from Saul, and an evil spirit from the Lord troubled him. And Saul's servants said unto him, Behold now, an evil spirit from God troubleth thee. Let our lord now command thy servants, which are before thee, to seek out a man, who is a cunning player on an harp: and it shall come to pass, when the evil spirit from God is upon thee, that he shall play with his hand, and thou shalt be well. And Saul said unto his servants, Provide me now a man that can play well, and bring him to me. Then answered*

one of the servants, and said, Behold, I have seen a son of Jesse the Bethlehemite, that is cunning in playing, and a mighty valiant man, and a man of war, and prudent in matters, and a comely person, and the Lord is with him. Wherefore Saul sent messengers unto Jesse, and said, Send me David thy son, which is with the sheep. And Jesse took an ass laden with bread, and a bottle of wine, and a kid, and sent them by David his son unto Saul. And David came to Saul, and stood before him: and he loved him greatly; and he became his armourbearer. And Saul sent to Jesse, saying, Let David, I pray thee, stand before me; for he hath found favour in my sight. And it came to pass, when the evil spirit from God was upon Saul, that David took an harp, and played with his hand: so Saul was refreshed, and was well, and the evil spirit departed from him.

1 Samuel 16:14-23

David carried a fresh anointing of worship that brought peace to Saul who was demonized because of his own rebellion. God is raising up a generation of David-type worshippers who have been alone in the field worshipping their King. They carry a powerful worship ministry that pushes back demonic forces.

There is a shift taking place in the Church right now. No longer can worship be just a casual experience. God is bringing forth prophetic songs that will change the spiritual climates of cities. God's people must break forth into another dimension of worship. It will sound different, feel different, and bring about different results. People who have not been bathed in prayer will not receive the minstrel's anointing; instead they will lash out because it is not what they expect.

Prophetic worship is a key tool in the fire of revival. The right songs will unlock anointings and release dimensions of heaven that will invade earth. Prophetic worship brings healing: spirit, body and soul. Prophetic worship empowers spiritual warfare and breaks the power of demon spirits!

> *Now Jericho was straitly shut up because of the children of Israel: none went out, and none came in. And the Lord said unto Joshua, See, I have given into thine hand Jericho, and the king thereof, and the mighty men of valour. And ye shall compass the city, all ye men of war, and go round about the city once. Thus shalt thou do six days. And seven priests shall bear before the ark seven trumpets of rams' horns: and the seventh day ye shall compass the city seven times, and the priests shall blow with the trumpets. And it shall come to pass, that when they make a long blast with the ram's horn, and when ye hear the sound of the trumpet, all the people shall shout with a great shout; and the wall of the city shall fall down flat, and the people shall ascend up every man straight before him.*
>
> *Joshua 6:1-5*

The walls of Jericho were defeating and resisting the plan of God for His children. The Lord gave specific instructions to surround the walls with praise and worship for the victory. He is anointing worship in this hour to destroy walls that have been designed to hold the people of God back. There is a breakthrough as we radically obey God in worship. God told the priests to blow the trumpets and the people to shout. He is raising a new standard of worship for this hour, for this time. There is a fire being placed in the spirits of end-time worship leaders.

By faith the walls of Jericho fell down, after they were compassed about seven days.

Hebrews 11:30

As Israel radically worshipped God, the walls came down. Revival worship is going to tear down the walls of religion over cities. God is calling forth prophetic psalmists to decree the song of the Lord and tear down the works of hell.

See, I have this day set thee over the nations and over the kingdoms, to root out, and to pull down, and to destroy, and to throw down, to build, and to plant.

Jeremiah 1:10

The prophetic ministry must tear down whatever is holding back the move of God. Revival worship empowers the tearing down of the devil's work and releases a wave of refreshing over the people of God. It is time to re-dig the wells of revival in worship. Worship forms a healing stream that will bring the bound to freedom.

But now bring me a minstrel. And it came to pass, when the minstrel played, that thehand of the Lord came upon him. And he said, Thus saith the Lord, Make this valley full of ditches. For thus saith the Lord, Ye shall not see wind, neither shall ye see rain; yet that valley shall be filled with water, that ye may drink, both ye, and your cattle, and your beasts. And this is but a light thing in the sight of the Lord: he will deliver the Moabites also into your hand. And ye shall smite every fenced city, and every choice city, and shall fell every good tree, and stop all wells of water, and mar every good piece of land with stones.

2 Kings 3:15-19

The king came to Elisha in search of prophetic direction. Elisha called for a minstrel to come and play. The minstrel's ministry released the Word of the Lord. Prophetic worship opens the territory to hear from heaven. It prepares the ground for the seed of the Word of the Lord. It causes the anointing of the Holy Spirit to flow in greater measures from the bellies of the servants of God.

Prophetic worship provides direction. As the minstrels sing the songs that God has given them for the hour, it brings clarity to what God is saying and doing. Prophetic worship unlocks the heavenlies and creates an atmosphere for supernatural miracles, prophetic ministry, and powerful proclamation of the Word of God.

We must be in sync with what the Holy Spirit is doing at this moment. As the new sounds come forth, they will be songs that we have never before heard. There will be levels of worship that corporately have never before been attained. We must not reject the ministry of end-time worship leaders because it is vital to bringing this revival forth.

If you are involved in worship ministry, you must take your place in the army. God is raising you up to bring His glory to the people. Spend much time seeking His face for direction, songs, and sounds. You hold the key to unlocking the wells of revival and letting the river flow. Do not let any man or religious devil bind you up. Obey God and be strong in the Lord.

5

Praying In The Peace Of God

True revival brings a dramatic shift. A person, city, or ministry is never the same after they have been consumed by revival's mighty flame. During an outpouring, God will often reveal people's spiritual assignments and positions. The enemy will be at work at the same time trying to pluck up that which has been planted by the hand of God.

The enemy uses a tremendously strong weapon in the mind called torment. He will torment people with thoughts of rejection, jealousy, memories of their past, and any other trick he can use. His purpose is to move them out of their assigned place. It is absolutely essential that every believer gets in the position God has for them so the revival fire can spread and influence the maximum number of people. It truly takes a dedicated army in order to lead revival.

Put on the whole armour of God, that ye may be able to stand against
the wiles of the devil.

Ephesians 6:11

The Bible instructs us to put on our armor and stand against the wiles *(schemes, tricks, strategies)* of the devil. Satan is not going to sit by and let the Church move into revival without giving us a fight. We do not have to fear him because we have been given all authority over him but we do need to recognize his tricks.

And I heard a loud voice saying in heaven, Now is come salvation,
and strength, and the kingdom of our God, and the power of his
Christ: for the accuser of our brethren is cast down, which accused
them before our God day and night.

Revelation 12:10

Satan hurls lying accusations at the minds of believers. This is one of his primary schemes. He will try to get right in the middle of the move of God and work on people's minds, bombarding them with lies.

For the weapons of our warfare are not carnal, but mighty through
God to the pulling down of strong holds;) Casting down imagina-
tions, and every high thing that exalteth itself against the knowledge
of God, and bringing into captivity every thought to the obedience of
Christ...

2 Corinthians 10:4-5

We do not have to climb to the high points of the city to deal with strongholds. The greatest strongholds are in the mind. Mental strongholds are systems, cycles, and patterns of thought attached to deception. The devil plants seeds through traumatic events and then your mind, which is like a computer, processes that information and forms a system of thought based upon it. This system of thought has the power to choke out the Word of God and your victory if you do not break it. Many people live bound by strongholds (*patterns of thought*) of fear, rejection, and shame. These are all tools of torment launched by the devil to keep the believer out of their destiny.

The Apostle Paul had experienced the personal defeats that come through soulish torment. He chronicled his experiences in Romans.

For that which I do I allow not: for what I would, that do I not; but what I hate, that do I. If then I do that which I would not, I consent unto the law that it is good. Now then it is no more I that do it, but sin that dwelleth in me. For I know that in me (that is, in my flesh,) dwelleth no good thing: for to will is present with me; but how to perform that which is good I find not. For the good that I would I do not: but the evil which I would not, that I do. Now if I do that I would not, it is no more I that do it, but sin that dwelleth in me, I find then a law, that, when I would do good, evil is present with me. For I delight in the law of God after the inward man: But I see another law in my members, warring against the law of my mind, and bringing me into captivity to the law of sin which is in my members. O wretched man that I am! who shall deliver me from the body of this death? I thank God through Jesus Christ our Lord. So then with the mind I myself serve The law of God; but with the flesh the law of sin.

Romans 7:19-25

Paul continued to struggle with sin. He felt defeated over and over again as sin pulled him into a dangerous lair. In order to understand this battle, we must review some basic principles:

Man is a spirit.

Man lives in a body.

Man has a soul (mind, will, and emotions).

And the very God of peace sanctify you wholly; and I pray God your whole spirit and soul and body be preserved blameless unto the coming of our Lord Jesus Christ.

1 Thessalonians 5:23

When we were born again, our spirit was re-made in the image and likeness of God. Our spirit has no appetite for sin or the things of this world. Our spirit has total and complete dominion because it is made in the image and the likeness of God Himself. Our flesh and mind did not get born again. In fact, our flesh has evil desires and nature living in it.

Now the works of the flesh are manifest, which are these; adultery, fornication, uncleanness, lasciviousness, idolatry, witchcraft, hatred, variance, emulations, wrath, strife, seditions, heresies, envyings, murders, drunkenness, revellings, and such like: of the which I tell you before, as I have also told you in time past, that they which do such things shall not inherit the kingdom of God.

Galatians 5:19-21

The way that we put the flesh under is by fasting and living out of our spirit. Fasting and prayer are power tools to deal with the works of the flesh. As a born-again believer, we are not bound by the flesh. Our mission is to walk in the new nature that dwells in the realm of the spirit. As we learn to walk in the law of the Spirit we become more and more free from the limitations of the flesh. Our mind must be renewed by getting in the Word of God and consistently reading, speaking, and meditating the written Word of God.

> *And be not conformed to this world: but be ye transformed by the renewing of your mind, that ye may prove what is that good, and acceptable, and perfect, will of God.*
>
> *Romans 12:2*

Sin was living in Paul's members (his flesh). He had total victory in the spirit. His battle was not with his inner man but his outer man (the soul and flesh). Many Christians face this same struggle. They have total victory in the spirit yet they yield to enduring cycles of defeat in the realm of their thought life. This is where sin lives in the life of a born-again child of God, in the flesh and soul.

Oftentimes, church members will get angry or offended by the actions of another believer. They point their finger at that person and proclaim that they knocked them off their destiny. Sometimes they will hop from church to church struggling with the same issues in a variety of different places. The real battle is not with the other people but the inner struggle in their unrenewed mind. When someone speaks to them in a certain manner they are instantly brought back to a place of pain and torment in their human mind.

If this cycle of torment is left alone they will never find spiritual success. There is a position within the peace of God that delivers the believer from the works of hell in the mental arena. As the fire of revival blazes in the Church, we must learn how to live in a supernatural peace that keeps us firmly planted in our spiritual assignments.

> *And your feet shod with the preparation of the gospel of peace.*
>
> *Ephesians 6:15*

In Paul's instructions to the Church about the armor of God he noted that our feet must be shod or covered in the gospel of peace. He gave this charge because our feet deal with assignment, authority, and position.

> *Every place that the sole of your foot shall tread upon, that have I given unto you, as I said unto Moses.*
>
> *Joshua 1:3*

We must live our lives planted in the supernatural peace of God. If our feet are not covered in peace they will go from place to place outside of the perfect will of God. When we get out of our assigned place we step out from under our spiritual assignment and anointing. We also relinquish our authority to the tormenter and allow him to persuade us.

Paul did not live his entire life struggling with his sinful flesh. He discovered a realm of prayer that is crucial if you are going to remain planted and be a part of God's revival army. The answer to his battle is revealed in the book of Romans.

There is therefore now no condemnation to them which are in Christ Jesus, who walk not after the flesh, but after the Spirit. For the law of the Spirit of life in Christ Jesus hath made me free from the law of sin and death. For what the law could not do, in that it was weak through the flesh, God sending his own Son in the likeness of sinful flesh, and for sin, condemned sin in the flesh: That the righteousness of the law might be fulfilled in us, who walk not after the flesh, but after the Spirit. For they that are after the flesh do mind the things of the flesh; but they that are after the Spirit the things of the Spirit.

Romans 8:1-5

Paul found a pathway out of the carnal nature. He discovered the walk of the Spirit. He was set totally free as he began to live out of his new nature and not yield to the dictates of sinful flesh.

God has provided for you and me a way to walk in such communion with Him that we are consumed by supernatural peace.

For to be carnally minded is death; but to be spiritually minded is life and peace. Because the carnal mind is enmity against God: for it is not subject to the law of God, neither indeed can be. So then they that are in the flesh cannot please God. But ye are not in the flesh, but in the Spirit, if so be that the Spirit of God dwell in you. Now if any man have not the Spirit of Christ, he is none of his. And if Christ be in you, the body is dead because of sin; but the Spirit is life because of righteousness.

Romans 8:6-10

Paul walked out of the limited dictates of his own righteousness and into the righteousness of faith. He walked out of sinful thinking and desires. He was delivered from carnal thinking and living. The law of sin became defeated in his life and he came to a place that the devil was unable to stop him because he had tapped so deeply into the law of the Spirit. How did Paul enter such peace?

> *Likewise the Spirit also helpeth our infirmities: for we know not what we should pray for as we ought: but the Spirit itself maketh intercession for us with groanings which cannot be uttered. And he that searcheth the hearts knoweth what is the mind of the Spirit, because he maketh intercession for the saints according to the will of God. And we know that all things work together for good to them that love God, to them who are the called according to his purpose.*
>
> *Romans 8:26-28*

Paul began to surrender to the powerful gift of praying in other tongues. When we pray in other tongues, the Holy Spirit begins to help our weaknesses. He goes right to the root of whatever is tormenting our minds and surrounds it with the Word of God. Then He prays through us to reveal the Word of God which releases faith (Romans 10:17) through the *rhema* (spoken or revealed) Word of God.

The Holy Spirit prays the absolute perfect will of God in our lives. God is orchestrating everything to our good, even as the devil plots behind the scenes to torment us and get our feet to move.

> *I thank my God, I speak with tongues more than ye all.*
>
> *1 Corinthians 14:18*

Paul came to a place in the Spirit in which he was constantly moving between tongues and his native language. This was the force that brought such powerful revelation alive in his spirit. He entered into the classroom of the Master Teacher (John 14:26) on a daily basis. Paul was transformed by his prayer life in the Spirit. He came to such a place of power that the devil could not destroy him. He only died when he willingly offered his life up to God.

You and I can come to that same place in the peace of God. This is key for the end-time revival. As the flames of revival burn brighter, the enemy will hurl accusations and torment at our human minds but we must be planted in the mind of the Spirit where supernatural peace dwells.

> *For with stammering lips and another tongue will he speak to this people. To whom he said, This is the rest wherewith ye may cause the weary to rest; and this is the refreshing: yet they would not hear.*
>
> *Isaiah 28:11-12*

Praying in the Holy Ghost will bring you to a place of rest. Your mind and heart become established in supernatural peace.

6

THE PERSONAL
MISSION OF REVIVAL

We often think of revival as a huge gathering of people or some massive event. True revival, however, begins with the very personal ministry of the Holy Spirit in the heart of a believer. As the believer presses into the things of God, a holy conviction grips their heart and the scales of sin begin to fall off their spiritual eyes.

> *And Ananias went his way, and entered into the house; and putting his hands on him said, Brother Saul, the Lord, even Jesus, that appeared unto thee in the way as thou camest, hath sent me, that thou mightest receive thy sight, and be filled with the Holy Ghost. And immediately there fell from his eyes as it had been scales: and he received sight forthwith, and arose, and was baptized. And when he had received meat, he was strengthened. Then was Saul certain days with the disciples which were at Damascus.*
>
> *Acts 9:17-19*

Saul had been blinded by the devil concerning the things of God. The god of this world attacks the minds of people and hardens their hearts to the gospel.

> *But if our gospel be hid, it is hid to them that are lost: In whom the god of this world hath blinded the minds of them which believe not, lest the light of the glorious gospel of Christ, who is the image of God, should shine unto them.*
>
> 2 Corinthians 4:3-4

We often wonder why certain regions or churches seem to be so cold to the things of God. Powerful preachers can come into their midst and not seem to get the results that they get preaching the same messages in other places. Why is this? It is because there are demonic assignments against the people of God. The devil has placed different types of spirits over particular regions in an attempt to hold back the move of God.

> *For we wrestle not against flesh and blood, but against principalities, against powers, against the rulers of the darkness of this world, against spiritual wickedness in high places.*
>
> Ephesians 6:12

If our spiritual eyes were opened we would see angels and demons traveling to and fro in the air space above our heads. We would also see ruling spirits that were given authority by men to occupy certain areas and influence them with the power of the devil. This is why particular regions face different struggles: perversion, poverty, religion, and the like. These struggles are the personalities of the spirits that have occupied that region. God has empowered His people to proclaim the gospel and set the captives free. We are not under the influence of any spirit except the Holy Spirit of God. We do not fear these demon spirits nor do we bow to their leadership. We bind them up and cast them out in the name of Jesus.

The fire of revival will burn away the strongholds that these devils have established in our churches and communities. People will be dramatically delivered as they enter into personal revival. God is calling forth a people who will fervently pursue the power and presence of the Holy Spirit and not be moved by anything that hell hurls their way.

The devil uses different schemes to hold back the move of God. In America, one of the primary tools that the enemy uses is financial prosperity and comfort. He lulls the Church to sleep by encouraging them to enjoy the things in the world more than the things of God. Money is a neutral force; it is neither good nor evil. It is the person who possesses the money that determines whether it be used for good or evil purposes. This is why the Bible teaches stewardship so strongly.

> *And he called his ten servants, and delivered them ten pounds, and said unto them, Occupy till I come.*
>
> Luke 19:13

Jesus instructed the Church to take control of financial resources and occupy until He comes. This is a Kingdom mindset. We can steward millions or even billions of dollars as long as we remain deeply rooted in the Kingdom. Sadly, many believers lose their focus as soon as they begin to enjoy a little bit of financial blessing.

Another tool of the devil against the work of revival is the spirit of religion. Religion paralyzes the power of God. Jesus rebuked the religious leaders because they were more concerned about maintaining their religious order than having a personal relationship with the Father. In my years of ministry, I have had more trouble out of this spirit than any other spirit. Countless times I have ministered the truth of God's Word to someone but they were so bound by the spirit of religion that they could not receive the freedom of that Word.

> *Woe unto you, scribes and Pharisees, hypocrites! for ye are like unto whited sepulchres, which indeed appear beautiful outward, but are within full of dead men's bones, and of all uncleanness.*
>
> *Matthew 23:27*

Religion is a monument-making spirit. It focuses on building large ornate monuments in places where God used to move. The revival anointing focuses on the fresh, living, breathing move of God. It is called a move of God because in the Spirit realm there is always a forward advance! Religious people camp out in what used to be; revival people are always pressing in the Spirit and seeking God for where He is going. Revival has a freshness about it.

Offense and criticism are two other key tools of the devil. I have always believed that everything we do in ministry should be backed by the Word of God and that we should strive to have a healthy balance of the Word and the Spirit in our ministries. It is very easy to get so far out in the spirit realm that a minister leaves the foundation of the Word and falls into error. That is why the Church must use the written Word as our measuring stick to prove what is of God and what is not.

There are people who will miss the fire of revival because they are so narrow-minded in their thinking. The ministry of Jesus was known for bold, radical, miracle-working encounters. You never knew what would happen if you hung around with Jesus. One day He was squaring off against the demoniac at Gadara and the next day He was raising Jairus' daughter from the dead. Jesus walked on water, spit in dirt to open blind eyes, and reattached an ear to a man's head. These were all unusual moves of God.

A critical spirit will cause believers to overlook the move of God because they are too busy finding fault. Again, let me reiterate that everything should be backed with the Word of God. There are, however, realms in the Spirit that are unknown to the typical church and believer. These realms are unlocked in the fire of revival and unusual things will begin to happen. These miracles are given as tools to win the lost.

The Church must be a place where people have God encounters! We should create such an atmosphere through worship, prayer, faith, and teaching that the things of the Spirit become tangible. There is an attack that the devil has brought against the Church of this hour to turn it away from the power of God. This is a false gospel. The gospel of Jesus Christ is built upon a foundation of power! No person in the Bible was saved without a transformation. They had a life-changing experience with the living Christ. Jesus wants to provide the same type of transforming miracles today. He is awakening His Bride to His awesome power and glory! It takes supernatural power to break bondages.

> *A brother offended is harder to be won than a strong city: and their contentions are like the bars of a castle.*
>
> Prov. 18:19

The revival move of God is one that is birthed in the Spirit and not the natural. As revival fire burns it will challenge believers to rise up and go higher in their walk with God. Those believers who are not staying in tune with God through prayer and in particular praying in the Spirit are targets for the spirit of offense. Offense will take a speck of truth and twist it into a massive demonic attack. Offense will also lie to the minds of believers, poisoning their thought lives.

One mark of revival is bold passion for God. Revival preaching will often confront sin and challenge the Church to lay down their lives. Revival demands that people press in and move deeper with God. Believers must guard their hearts against the spirit of offense because it will shut down the personal work of revival.

> *Create in me a clean heart, O God; and renew a right spirit within me. Cast me not away from thy presence; and take not thy holy spirit from me. Restore unto me the joy of thy salvation; and uphold me with thy free spirit.*
>
> Psalm 51:10-12

In order to experience the deep cleansing work of revival, we must strive to keep our hearts established in God. We need God's love working in us so we can effectively love our brothers and sisters. Each day we must enter into the presence of God and spend time allowing the Holy Spirit to search our hearts and cleanse us from any wrong thoughts or motives.

Every day in our prayer time we need to come before God and examine our hearts. We need to loose forgiveness over everyone who has hurt us. We need to develop the fruit of the Holy Spirit by spending time with Him. As we press into God, we must also resist any prideful spirit and stay humble. In order to be humble, we must be transparent before others and be quick to repent.

> *Confess your faults one to another, and pray one for another, that ye may be healed. The effectual fervent prayer of a righteous man availeth much.*
>
> *James 5:16*

If the Lord quickens in your spirit that you have hurt someone or acted in a manner that doesn't please Him, go to that person immediately and get it right! I have had to do this many times through the years and it is tough but it keeps us on the right path. Recently, I was ministering under a very heavy anointing and I said something a little harsh to one of our volunteers; immediately the Holy Spirit checked my spirit. He told me to repent before the whole crowd! I did not want to do it but it is better to obey God than man, so I did it. We are all in this exciting move together and we need each other so we must walk in love and humility.

As the fire of revival blazes forward, we must never forget that its most powerful effect is not on a stadium of people but on the heart of a single believer. Revival has an intimate purpose, to re-ignite every heart with a burning passion for God. Revival draws each person back to their first love.

7

CONSUMING FIRE

For our God is a consuming fire.
Hebrews 12:29

One of the most prominent characteristics of revival is the consuming fire of God. People who have been involved in revival often testify of becoming so alive to the things of God that they struggle just to go through the mundane routine of normal life.

As the fire of revival flows over people they are supernaturally overwhelmed by the Spirit of the Lord. The fire of God saturates every part of their being: *spirit, soul, and body.* This is why many revivals report unusual physical reactions such as jerking, trembling, laughing, and weeping, just to name a few. These reactions are the result of the body coming in contact with the blazing fire of God.

Imagine for a moment a forest full of beautiful trees that is suddenly devastated by a large wild fire. The statuesque trees are instantly transformed to mere piles of smoldering ash. You can no longer see any resemblance of a forest. All that remains is a desolate place covered in ash.

In the same manner, the fire of revival is a consuming force. As the flames spread, fear, sin, lust, pride, rebellion, and many other bondages are destroyed. Where there was once a large stronghold, there now is freedom. You can no longer see any form of that bondage because it has been overtaken by God's holy fire. His fire is transformative and full of delivering power. In a moment, the fire of God takes you from just hearing about a move of God into experiencing that move. This fire also releases a deep passion on the inside of your spirit man. As you are in the presence of revival fire, you are stirred in the deepest part of your being.

> *And above the firmament that was over their heads was the likeness of a throne, as the appearance of a sapphire stone: and upon the likeness of the throne was the likeness as the appearance of a man above upon it. And I saw as the colour of amber, as the appearance of fire round about within it, from the appearance of his loins even upward, and from the appearance of his loins even downward, I saw as it were the appearance of fire, and it had brightness round about. As the appearance of the bow that is in the cloud in the day of rain, so was the appearance of the brightness round about. This was the appearance of the likeness of the glory of the LORD. And when I saw it, I fell upon my face, and I heard a voice of one that spake.*
>
> *Ezekiel 1:26-28*

Ezekiel had a vision of the Lord of Glory. The fire of revival is the revelation of the Lord Himself. In revival moves, God comes down in the midst of the people in full manifestation. Strange and unusual manifestations take place and what was once difficult suddenly becomes easy in the presence of the Creator.

The Lord is clothed in fire. It is impossible to enter into the manifest presence of God without experiencing the fire of God. The fire is in the Holy Place. Outer-court Christians *(those who have been converted but live in the flesh)* will not be able to experience the fullness of the fire of God. That fire burns in the Holy Place. It is revealed to those who have laid down their lives and moved beyond the flesh realm into the realm of the Spirit.

> *I beseech you therefore, brethren, by the mercies of God, that ye present your bodies a living sacrifice, holy, acceptable unto God, which is your reasonable service. And be not conformed to this world: but be ye transformed by the renewing of your mind, that ye may prove what is that good, and acceptable, and perfect, will of God.*
>
> *Romans 12:1-2*

Paul's admonition to the church at Rome was to lay their very lives on the altar and become a living sacrifice. The altar is the place of fire and the place of death. There is a level of Christianity that much of the modern-day Church does not know. It is that place where you have surrendered your entire existence to God. As the believer approaches the fire of God, it means certain death to the life of the flesh but a deep release of the life of the Spirit.

> *And when he had called the people unto him with his disciples also, he said unto them, Whosoever will come after me, let him deny himself, and take up his cross, and follow me.*
>
> *Mark 8:34*

Jesus instructed His followers to deny themselves. This message has been abandoned in many Christian circles today. The gospel is still the same. God is looking for a people who will follow after Him with reckless abandon. He wants to place His dreams and His desires in our hearts. This is the spirit of surrender that God wants to grip the Church. He desires His children to be so obedient to Him that they will minister to any person, at anytime, in any place.

God wants to send His children on Holy Ghost rescue missions. There are people stuck in the mire of sin and bondage that need to be broken loose by the power of God. All it takes is one obedient believer to hear from heaven and go minister to that bound person and they can be set free. As we move deeper into the consuming fire, we will become radically submitted vessels through which God can pour out His saving and delivering power!

The devil has distracted much of the Church and pulled them away from sacrifice and obedience. Revival fire is calling the Church back to the altar, back to the place of holy living, and back to radical obedience.

> *For if ye live after the flesh, ye shall die: but if ye through the Spirit do mortify the deeds of the body, ye shall live. For as many as are led by the Spirit of God, they are the sons of God.*
>
> *Romans 8:13-14*

The walk of the Spirit takes you to a place of victory over the flesh. How many members of the Body of Christ struggle with hearing from God and being led by the Holy Spirit? Many Christians are not confident that they are being led by God, yet this is one of the most basic elements of Christianity. Why is this?

One reason that this struggle has gripped the Church is because the Church has become mired in a powerless gospel that is self-serving and flesh-empowering. We must receive a dramatic deliverance from certain methods and theologies running through today's Church. The Body of Christ must receive the ministry of the Holy Spirit. God wants to do things in the midst of His people. He sent the Holy Spirit to us as our Helper and still many churches have shunned the life-giving ministry of the Holy Spirit.

The Christian who is living their life surrendered to the fire and dying to the flesh is sensitive to the voice of the Spirit. When you have been purged in the fire you are quick to obey God.

And he said unto me, Son of man, stand upon thy feet, and I will speak unto thee. And the spirit entered into me when he spake unto me, and set me upon my feet, that I heard him that spake unto me. And he said unto me, Son of man, I send thee to the children of Israel, to a rebellious nation that hath rebelled against me: they and their fathers have transgressed against me, even unto this very day.

Ezekiel 2:1-3

After the fire of God had overwhelmed Ezekiel, God gave him prophetic instructions. The fire of revival carries prophetic instruction. God speaks in the midst of fire! When He revealed Himself to Moses it was in the burning bush. God called to Moses and reminded him of his prophetic destiny.

And when Paul had gathered a bundle of sticks, and laid them on the fire, there came a viper out of the heat, and fastened on his hand.

Acts 28:3

The fire of God draws out vipers! When God's fire is turned up in a church, devils will be exposed. The Church must just remain in a spirit of prayer and not be moved by the enemy. Devils will try to attack you when you press into the fire. The purpose of the attack is to get you out of the fire of God. The devil is ruthless. He will use anybody including your family, friends, or fellow church members. This is why you must be prayed up every day and walking according to the marching orders that the Holy Spirit has given you. There is no time to be distracted, not even for a moment.

When you press into the fire of God, attacks and persecution will come but you must shake it off. God has supernaturally empowered you to rise up and win. That viper should have killed Paul but Paul was not a normal man. He was a child of God Almighty. He shook that devil off and moved on unharmed.

Neither give place to the devil.

Ephesians 4:27

We must close every door to the devil so we can keep going forth into the fire. God will quicken in our spirit those things or people we need to stay away from. Be quick to obey Him and don't give the devil an inch.

And it came to pass, as we went to prayer, a certain damsel possessed with a spirit of divination met us, which brought her masters much gain by soothsaying: The same followed Paul and us, and cried, saying, These men are the servants of the most high God, which shew unto us the way of salvation. And this did she many days. But Paul, being grieved, turned and said to the spirit, I command thee in the name of Jesus Christ to come out of her. And he came out the same hour. And when her masters saw that the hope of their gains was gone, they caught Paul and Silas, and drew them into the market-place unto the rulers, And brought them to the magistrates, saying, These men, being Jews, do exceedingly trouble our city, And teach customs, which are not lawful for us to receive, neither to observe, being Romans. And the multitude rose up together against them: and the magistrates rent off their clothes, and commanded to beat them. And when they had laid many stripes upon them, they cast them into prison, charging the jailor to keep them safely: Who, having received such a charge, thrust them into the inner prison, and made their feet fast in the stocks.

Acts 16:16-24

Paul cast the spirit of the devil out of that young lady and turned the city upside down! When you are full of the fire of God, you will cause trouble for the devil. The devil loves weak, luke-warm, religious Christians who are not engaged in any ministry that challenges his kingdom. He doesn't mind a bit of we go to church and sing songs as long as we don't trouble him. But when a Christian is filled with the radical fire of God, they will trouble the devil.

The day is upon us that the Church must rise up and reclaim our communities. We need to say, "No" to drug addiction, homo-sexuality, psychic witches, and palm readers. God has given us the authority in the land and we must exercise it in the name of Jesus. Those filled with the fire of God will take on the demonic forces without fear.

And when they found them not, they drew Jason and certain brethren unto the rulers of the city, crying, These that have turned the world upside down are come hither also.

Acts 17:6

The Early Church was on fire and they turned their world upside down. The Church in this hour is going to turn this world upside down with the power and fire of God. The army of the Lord is going to go forth and claim nations and generations for God. This is an hour of radical revival fire. As your heart becomes consumed, you will step out in faith and refuse to be silent anymore.

Those touched by the fire of God do not care what the world says! The world did not understand the ministry of Jesus. While many received Him, many others became violently offended by Him. The world mocked the outpouring of the Spirit in Acts chapter two. They could not understand the things of the Spirit because they were locked in a prison of the flesh. The world will not understand the revival fire that burns in the hearts of God's people but we must be delivered from their opinions. There are those who are broken, hurting, and living in darkness, waiting for a messenger burning with the fire of God to come. You are a part of the army that will go.

The fire of revival ultimately prepares the believer to fulfill their assignment. Once you have passed through the fire of God, you are cleansed, filled with fresh passion, and ready to impact the world. Revival spreads much like a natural fire. It is passed from person to person, church to church, and ministry to ministry. All it takes is a spark to ignite a raging revival inferno that will shake a city.

Revival shifts people into their assignments and destiny. When revival hits a church, that church receives instruction in the midst of fire to impact their city. Not only do instructions come in the midst of fire but also the power of God comes to carry out the instruction.

Fire sends you into the mission field. Souls are the prize of revival. God ignites the believers, calls them back to their first love, and then sends them into the lost and broken world with His holy fire.

8

POWER TEAMS

In the traditional model of ministry, a lone man or woman faithfully builds a ministry and then begins to serve the Body of Christ through their particular gifting. Depending on the size and reach of their ministry, they reach a certain number of people with the gospel. As the fire of revival begins to consume this generation, there is a paradigm shift upon us. Anointed men and women will still have their own life-giving ministries but there will be a partnering of the various gifts in order to shake cities. Apostles will be linked with Prophets. Teachers will join forces with Evangelists. We will begin to see a more complete picture of Christ as all five ministry gifts flow, joining into one sweeping river of revival.

In this revival time, God is drawing people together by His Spirit to achieve a common goal. Real Revivalists do not care about getting the credit or receiving the accolades of man. Instead they long to see the dynamite power of God breaking down the strongholds of the devil. This is an hour of divine partnership by the Spirit.

We having the same spirit of faith, according as it is written, I believed, and therefore have I spoken; we also believe, and therefore speak.

2 Corinthians 4:13

Power teams are comprised of people who share the same spirit of faith. Together these teams will be a part of regional transformation. They operate in the God kind of faith as they see the vision and heart of God for the city. They then prophesy and declare revival over that territory.

Jesus understood the concept of team ministry. One of the ministries in which He devoted most of His time was the calling, training, and development of His twelve disciples. Before appointing His ministry team, His inner circle, He spent time praying! Prayer and being led by the Spirit is the key to forming healthy ministry relationships. After Jesus had prayed, He called forth the twelve.

And he goeth up into a mountain, and calleth unto him whom he would: and they came unto him. And he ordained twelve, that they should be with him, and that he might send them forth to preach, And to have power to heal sicknesses, and to cast out devils:

Mark 3:13-15

Jesus, the Son of God, worked with a power team. He gave us a pattern of ministry that includes team work. It takes various giftings, ministries, and anointings to spread the flame of revival in an effective manner. Jesus never sent anyone to minister alone, instead He commissioned power teams to go forth and take the gospel message to the hurting.

Then he called his twelve disciples together, and gave them power and authority over all devils, and to cure diseases. And he sent them to preach the kingdom of God, and to heal the sick.

Luke 9:1-2

After these things the Lord appointed other seventy also, and sent them two and two before his face into every city and place, whither he himself would come.

Luke 10:1

Jesus recognized the need for partnership in ministry. In this final move of God every gift is needed in order to get the job done and manifest the fullness of Christ. Not only is every gift needed but every gift needs the other in order to be effective.

And he said unto them, Go ye into all the world, and preach the gospel to every creature. He that believeth and is baptized shall be saved; but he that believeth not shall be damned. And these signs shall follow them that believe; In my name shall they cast out devils; they shall speak with new tongues; They shall take up serpents; and if they drink any deadly thing, it shall not hurt them; they shall lay hands on the sick, and they shall recover.

Mark 16:15-18

The last thing that Jesus did before He left this earth to be reunited with the Father was to commission *every* believer to join His power team. There is not one person who has all the answers. It takes the full Body of Christ working together to get the job done.

For too long there have been people in the ministry and in the Church who have the attitude that they have arrived! They thought that they were the all-inclusive, the only man or woman with everything the Church needed. This is a deceiving spirit. If we attempt to do all the work on our own we will give way to a prideful spirit and the devil will set us up for a fall.

> *Pride goeth before destruction, and an haughty spirit before a fall. Better it is to be of an humble spirit with the lowly, than to divide the spoil with the proud.*
>
> *Proverbs 16:18-19*

> *Now there were in the church that was at Antioch certain prophets and teachers; as Barnabas, and Simeon that was called Niger, and Lucius of Cyrene, and Manaen, which had been brought up with Herod the tetrarch, and Saul. As they ministered to the Lord, and fasted, the Holy Ghost said, Separate me Barnabas and Saul for the work whereunto I have called them. And when they had fasted and prayed, and laid their hands on them, they sent them away.*
>
> *Acts 13:1-3*

Prayer and ministry were team efforts in the Early Church. The Prophets and Teachers were not doing their own thing. They were binding together in prayer, seeking the plan of God for the Church. It was in the midst of team prayer that God revealed the destinies of Paul and Barnabas. As power teams come together in the fire of revival, divine revelation of spiritual assignments will come forth!

Paul launched His ministry with a God-given ministry partner (Barnabas). He later traveled with Silas.

And Paul chose Silas, and departed, being recommended by the brethren unto the grace of God.

Acts 15:40

Paul also took Timothy with him as one of his disciples:

Then came he to Derbe and Lystra: and, behold, a certain disciple was there, named Timotheus, the son of a certain woman, which was a Jewess, and believed; but his father was a Greek: Which was well reported of by the brethren that were at Lystra and Iconium. Him would Paul have to go forth with him; and took and circumcised him because of the Jews which were in those quarters: for they knew all that his father was a Greek.

Acts 16:1-3

From whom the whole body fitly joined together and compacted by that which every joint supplieth, according to the effectual working in the measure of every part, maketh increase of the body unto the edifying of itself in love.

Ephesians 4:16

As the ministry gifts work together, they strengthen and sharpen each other. The Apostle can draw inspiration and prophetic unction from the Prophet. This encounter will launch both ministry gifts into a deeper and more meaningful realm of ministry.

Too often the devil deceives believers into thinking that their gift is ineffective. This is a lie of the enemy intended to hinder the move of God. Each ministry grace is important for the overall success in the plan of God for a given city. For example, if the ministry of helps team is not prayed up and in position then the five-fold ministry gifts will grow weary and frustrated, lacking the support necessary to bring in the harvest. If the intercessors are not raised up to provide the spark of revival then the fire will not be able to burn in the manner God intended.

We, as believers, must confidently know that God created each of us and marked us with unique purpose. As the fire of revival burns, we will be shifted by God and spiritual leadership into the position that God has ordained for us. We must resist feelings of inadequacy and insignificance. We must also develop the fruit of patience so we will not allow ourselves to move before the timing of God.

God knows exactly who to partner you with in revival. You may feel alone and frustrated but you have a place on a power team. God is preparing you for that place. Build a foundation of prayer in your life and God will lead you to the right place, at the right time, with the right people!

> *Now when the apostles which were at Jerusalem heard that Samaria had received the word of God, they sent unto them Peter and John: Who, when they were come down, prayed for them, that they might receive the Holy Ghost:*
>
> *Acts 8:14-15*

Philip, the Evangelist, had traveled to Samaria and brought the fire of revival. The entire city was shaken by a radical move of God that was comprised of bold preaching along with miracles, signs, and wonders. The office of an Evangelist carries a heavy flow of the miraculous. In fact, a traveling ministry who claims the office of an Evangelist but does not operate in miracles and healings is either a Teacher or an exhorter.

Evangelists are equipped by God to start fires but they are not builders or Teachers. When the Apostles heard about the revival that Philip sparked, they recognized the need to establish the new converts in doctrinal truth. Philip was not offended or haughty, but recognized the need for Holy Ghost back up and welcomed the Apostle's ministry.

Another realm of power teams is impartation, activation, and equipping.

> *For the perfecting of the saints, for the work of the ministry, for the edifying of the body of Christ:*
>
> *Ephesians 4:12*

The ministry gifts equip the saints for the work of the ministry. As believers join up with teams, they find new levels of ministry and spiritual gifting. The right people, carrying the right ministry grace, will unlock certain realms and levels of your spiritual life.

> *For I long to see you, that I may impart unto you some spiritual gift, to the end ye may be established.*
>
> *Romans 1:11*

Five-fold ministry gifts make spiritual deposits into the lives of believers. Being a part of the right power team will release a divine flow of anointing and grace into your life.

As God brings His ministers together to partner in revival, there will be an explosive effect in the Spirit along with a dynamic atmosphere for spiritual growth. Each gift will pull the other up higher in the things of God.

> *Paul, an apostle of Jesus Christ by the will of God, according to the promise of life which is in Christ Jesus, To Timothy, my dearly beloved son: Grace, mercy, and peace, from God the Father and Christ Jesus our Lord.*
>
> *2 Timothy 1:1-2*

After Timothy traveled with the Apostle Paul, he became his spiritual son. Timothy's life was never the same because he was a part of Paul's power team. God has placed certain people in my life who had something in their belly that I needed to launch me into my destiny. The most powerful ministry relationship that I have ever had is with my spiritual father, Dr. Norvel Hayes. God sent me to his Bible College when I was only seventeen years old. God knew that I needed the revelation of faith that rested upon his ministry. I began as a student but am now a spiritual son who has had the privilege to serve alongside of Dr. Hayes and his daughter, Zona, in their ministry. God allowed me to cut my spiritual teeth under a giant of the faith!

> *Wherefore I put thee in remembrance that thou stir up the gift of God, which is in thee by the putting on of my hands.*
>
> *2 Timothy 1:6*

Paul's ministry deposited spiritual gifts into Timothy's life. Power teams will bring a deposit into the spirits of those on the teams.

God knows who has in their belly what is needed to launch you into new realms of power and ministry. It is not that we place our eyes upon men or women. We understand that all blessings come from God but He uses His servants in our spiritual development.

The people of God will no longer just be spectators but will take their place as end-time harvesters. The Body of Christ will rise into maturity as they are equipped by the five fold-ministry gifts.

9

THE REVIVAL ARMY

The wind of God and the breath of God in the Bible represents the life of God.

The hand of the Lord was upon me, and carried me out in the spirit of the Lord, and set me down in the midst of the valley which was full of bones, And caused me to pass by them round about: and, behold, there were very many in the open valley; and, lo, they were very dry. And he said unto me, Son of man, can these bones live? And I answered, O Lord God, thou knowest. Again he said unto me, Prophesy upon these bones, and say unto them, O ye dry bones, hear the word of the Lord. Thus saith the Lord God unto these bones; Behold, I will cause breath to enter into you, and ye shall live: And I will lay sinews upon you, and will bring up flesh upon you, and cover you with skin, and put breath in you, and ye shall live; and ye shall know that I am the Lord. So I prophesied as I was commanded: and as I prophesied, there was a noise, and behold a shaking, and the bones came together, bone to his bone. And when I beheld, lo, the sinews and the flesh came up upon them, and the skin covered them above: but there was no breath in them. Then said he unto me, Prophesy unto the wind, prophesy, son of man, and say to the wind, Thus saith the Lord God; Come from the four winds, O breath, and breathe upon these slain, that they may live. So I prophesied as he commanded me, and the breath came into them, and they lived, and stood up upon their feet, an exceeding great army.

Ezekiel 37:1-10

And the Lord God formed man of the dust of the ground, and breathed into his nostrils the breath of life; and man became a living soul.

Genesis 2:7

In the account of man's creation, God breathed life into us. At that moment, the Spirit of God came into the dust and life was born.

In the beginning God created the heaven and the earth.

And the earth was without form, and void; and darkness was upon the face of the deep. And the Spirit of God moved upon the face of the waters.

Genesis 1:1-2

The Hebrew word for *spirit* is *ruach*, which means "air in motion." It is the same word for "breath." It also means "life." In the account of creation, the breath of God was hovering on the face of a formless earth. Then God began to speak! As He spoke, breath *(wind, ruach, spirit)* was released. God's spoken word came through His breath just as when we speak. His breath and wind changed the molecular structure of earth and life came forth along with divine order.

> *And when the day of Pentecost was fully come, they were all with one accord in one place. And suddenly there came a sound from heaven as of a rushing mighty wind, and it filled all the house where they were sitting. And there appeared unto them cloven tongues like as of fire, and it sat upon each of them.*
>
> *Acts 2:1-3*

When the Holy Spirit was poured out in the upper room, the disciples heard and felt a wind! Why? They heard it because the breath of God came and created a fire. As the wind of God hit that place, fire began to break forth in the spirits of the people and they were overtaken by the power of God.

In the same way, God is breathing upon His Church at this moment. He is releasing His creative word along with His breath and supernatural power is coming forth. As the wind blows upon revival sparks, they will erupt into wild fires which will consume churches, cities, regions, schools, and campuses.

Many churches in this hour have become so natural that they are full of carnal life and void of the presence of God. There is a holy wind blowing across the nations of the world, calling the mighty army of God to arise and take the land.

God is the Master Planner. He has ordained a position for every person in His last-day plan. The enemy will do all that he can to get each of us out of that plan but he is no match for the power of God. If we will flow with the blowing of the wind of God, then we will be picked up out of "normal" Christianity and swept into the rushing winds of God.

Leading this army will be men and women who have been locked away in the presence of God. Many of these last-day Revivalists have been rejected by the religious establishment. While Christian leaders have failed to embrace their ministries, they have been on the backside of the desert worshipping God and He has deposited the seeds of revival in their spirits.

Now when they saw the boldness of Peter and John, and perceived that they were unlearned and ignorant men, they marvelled; and they took knowledge of them, that they had been with Jesus. And beholding the man which was healed standing with them, they could say nothing against it. But when they had commanded them to go aside out of the council, they conferred among themselves, Saying, What shall we do to these men? for that indeed a notable miracle hath been done by them is manifest to all them that dwell in Jerusalem; and we cannot deny it .

Acts 4:13-16

Peter and John were being persecuted by the religious leaders of their day. Yet, in the middle of the persecution, the power of God was seen. Revivalists are people who know how to move in the power of God. It was evident to the people that Peter and John had been in the presence of God.

Many years ago the Lord showed me the days that lay ahead. He told me that there was coming a time when men would celebrate other men who had accomplished big things in Christian ministry. He then showed me Revivalists who were so full of the glory of God that His power emanated from their physical being. He told me to look for the glory and partner with ministers who had the glory of God.

I saw in my spirit a separation that would come. I did not understand it at that time but I do now. He was revealing to me that many churches would abandon spiritual ministry in exchange for soulish programs. He told me to stay away from that type of ministry and stick with the gospel. It is only the power of the gospel that can fill empty lives, heal broken hearts, and deliver tormented minds.

Much of the Church world is dry and empty. We have had plenty of big achievements and seen the success of the ideas of men. Still, we long for something more. Our spirits were created to be filled with the very life and presence of God. God wants nothing less for us than the full weight of His glory being revealed in us. He is raising up a remnant of ministers who do not care about money, titles, or fame but just want His glory. These are the end-time Revivalists who will bring the fire of revival to regions, nations, churches, and people everywhere.

Revivalists are men and women who are absolutely filled to overflowing with the fire of God.

Then the Lord put forth his hand, and touched my mouth. And the Lord said unto me, Behold, I have put my words in thy mouth.

Jeremiah 1:9

God has filled the mouth of these Revivalists with fire. They refuse to preach the words of men, instead choosing to hear from heaven and declare the very oracles of God. As they preach and prophesy there is a fire in their bellies. They are carriers of the torch of the Lord, spreading His flame from place to place.

Revivalists are not afraid to confront lukewarm spirits in the Church. There are many ministers in this hour who have traded their call for religious politics. Instead of standing up and declaring the Word of the Lord, they spend their time satisfying men.

The voice of revival is the voice of reform. False methodologies and religious practices must be exposed in order to enter into true revival. Those bound with the spirit of religion will call these Revivalists mean spirited, judgmental preachers. What the Church must understand is that there are spirits sent against the Body of Christ to quench the power of God. We are not called as leaders to war against our brothers and sisters but we are accountable to God to proclaim the truth and expose wicked spiritual forces. If we sit back and remain silent then we shall be judged as unfaithful to the call of God. Our battle is not in the natural but in the spirit.

For we wrestle not against flesh and blood, but against principalities, against powers, against the rulers of the darkness of this world, against spiritual wickedness in high places.

Ephesians 6:12

For I know this, that after my departing shall grievous wolves enter in among you, not sparing the flock. Also of your own selves shall men arise, speaking perverse things, to draw away disciples after

them. Therefore watch, and remember, that by the space of three years
I ceased not to warn every one night and day with tears.

Acts 20:29-31

Paul was a bold voice of truth to his spiritual sons and daughters. He repeatedly warned them that the devil was going to come to rend them not only from outside but also from within! This new generation of Revivalists is mandated by God to reveal the hindering spirits and doctrines of men that are holding back the fullness of the Holy Spirit. Paul even spoke specifically about ministers that were involved in false doctrine.

Holding faith, and a good conscience; which some having put away
concerning faith have made shipwreck: Of whom is Hymenaeus and
Alexander; whom I have delivered unto Satan, that they may learn
not to blaspheme.

1 Timothy 1:19-20

It is the ministry assignment of Apostles, Prophets, Teachers, and Pastors to equip the Church with truth. Part of that process is revealing non-biblical practices. When we stand and preach against fornication, those who believe the Bible will agree. Yet, when we proclaim that lukewarm churches and certain spiritual practices don't obey the Bible and are wrong, some Christians get angry. They think that we are being judgmental and critical. Both Jesus and Paul boldly spoke out against the religious practices of their day. They saw every religious practice that led people away from truth as an enemy of freedom and salvation.

God is asking His revival army to stand up and reclaim the land with the full gospel. The powerless practices of the seeker-friendly movement and other lukewarm methodologies are lowering the bar for a generation of ministers. These preachers are not our enemies, they are our friends and as friends we are responsible to speak the truth to them in love. At the end of the day, we are judged by an audience of one, Jesus the Righteous King. If we stay silent to please the religious devils and disobey God, then we will be very sad on the day of our appearance before the King.

We must show the Church world why these lukewarm doctrines are wrong. These practices are not anywhere in the Bible. Not one New Testament minister built his whole ministry without power and preaching. Nevertheless, in today's Church ministers often refuse to preach certain Biblical truths for fear of man. We must raise the bar and restore the gospel ministry to this generation. **It is time to stand up, speak out, and press in!**

Revivalists must have an intense relationship with the Holy Spirit. It is impossible to move in the fire of revival without being in tune with the Holy Spirit and His ministry. This is one vital mark of revival ministry.

> *And my speech and my preaching was not with enticing words of man's wisdom, but in demonstration of the Spirit and of power.*
>
> *1 Corinthians 2:4*

Revivalists must not simply preach messages but must move in the power and demonstration of the Spirit. Much of the modern Church has become lazy in faith and doesn't press in for manifestations of the realm of the Spirit. Jesus told us that it was His will that the manifestation (making visible) of the Spirit would be available to every man (1 Corinthians 12:7).

Revivalists are called by God to re-ignite the passion for the move of the Holy Spirit in the Church. The Holy Spirit desires to come alongside of the declared Word and bring signs and wonders.

There are two important facets of the revival army that God is raising up. There are those new breed ministers touched by God to lead this mighty move; then there are the intercessors, psalmists, givers, ministers of helps, and gifts of governments who will work alongside of the five-fold ministers to usher in the move of God.

It is imperative that you allow God's fire to be activated in your life and ministry so you do not miss revival fire. God has a plan and you are a vital part of that plan. He has strategically created you and ordained a Kingdom purpose for your life.

10

REVIVAL CENTERS

G od is birthing a desire inside of ministry leaders to abandon the normal way of doing things and press in to experience the fire of revival in their churches and ministries. This will mean a shift in the thinking and attitudes of the people who are a part of these ministries. No longer can we be content just to have services void of the presence of God. Our heart's cry must be that God would come and fill the Church with His manifest presence, glory, and power!

In the year that king Uzziah died I saw also the Lord sitting upon a throne, high and lifted up, and his train filled the temple. Above it stood the seraphims: each one had six wings; with twain he covered his face, and with twain he covered his feet, and with twain he did fly. And one cried unto another, and said, Holy, holy, holy, is the Lord of hosts: the whole earth is full of his glory. And the posts of the door moved at the voice of him that cried, and the house was filled with smoke. Then said I, Woe is me! for I am undone; because I am a man of unclean lips, and I dwell in the midst of a people of unclean lips: for mine eyes have seen the King, the Lord of hosts. Then flew one of the seraphims unto me, having a live coal in his hand, which he had taken with the tongs from off the altar: And he laid it upon my mouth, and said, Lo, this hath touched thy lips; and thine iniquity is taken away, and thy sin purged. Also I heard the voice of the Lord, saying, Whom shall I send, and who will go for us? Then said I, Here am I; send me.

Isaiah 6:1-8

God wants to come and occupy every place of worship with His majestic power. This is an hour of the supernatural. We will encounter angels, see visions, and dream dreams on an unprecedented level. God has planned an almighty outpouring in the final age to awaken the Church and shake the nations.

No longer can we measure success by natural means. For too long Pastors and ministry leaders have spent the majority of their time counting people and money. While many ministers have built vast enterprises, they have also lost the life-changing presence of God. Services with no miracles or radical deliverances have become common. The supernatural ministry of the Holy Spirit has been choked out of many churches and replaced with a succeed-at-all-costs mentality. Churches have reformed and become more like corporations and less like holy houses of worship. Let me be clear, I believe in big blessings, radical success, and abundant financial provision, but not in place of the move of God. If a church sets its face to seek God with all of its strength, then the ministry will be blessed both spiritually and naturally.

There is a radical reform coming in the Church. Revival centers are being birthed around the globe. They are being sent by God to ignite the flame of revival in the hearts of people. A generation is being called higher. God is asking His servants to embrace the fire and glory of God.

And unto the angel of the church of the Laodiceans write; These things saith the Amen, the faithful and true witness, the beginning of the creation of God; I know thy works, that thou art neither cold nor hot: I would thou wert cold or hot. So then because thou art lukewarm, and neither cold nor hot, I will spue thee out of my mouth. Because thou sayest, I am rich, and increased with goods, and have need of nothing; and knowest not that thou art wretched, and miserable, and poor, and blind, and naked: I counsel thee to buy of me gold tried in the fire, that thou mayest be rich; and white raiment, that thou mayest be clothed, and that the shame of thy nakedness do not appear; and anoint thine eyes with eyesalve, that thou mayest see. As many as I love, I rebuke and chasten: be zealous therefore, and repent. Behold, I stand at the door, and knock: if any man hear my voice, and open the door, I will come in to him, and will sup with him, and he with me. To him that overcometh will I grant to sit with me in my throne, even as I also overcame, and am set down with my Father in his throne. He that hath an ear, let him hear what the Spirit saith unto the churches.

Revelation 3:14-22

Revival centers are places ordained by God to call people forth out of lukewarm Christianity. There are people going to church every week and still never experiencing the transforming power of the gospel. These revival churches are places of divine change.

The religious will hate the revival churches. They will mock, persecute, and attack churches full of revival power. This is the same spirit that mocked Jesus and attacked Paul. The intercessors will pull down the words of the devil in prayer. This is why the fire of intercession is so important in revival centers. It is the prayers of the people of God that turn the assignments of hell away.

Those who are called to be a part of a revival church or ministry must stay built up in faith. It is the shield of faith that quenches the fiery darts of the enemy. If we keep our faith strong then the devil's weapons will be ineffective against us.

Jesus is standing at the door of the Church and knocking. The Scripture in Revelation three says that He wants to come in. This was not written to the world but to the Church. Many churches have locked Jesus out and that is why they have become lukewarm. He desires to come and fellowship with His people. He wants His glory to rest in churches and shake entire communities. Revival churches and ministries do not seek to fulfill their own agenda.

> *Jesus answered them, and said, My doctrine is not mine, but his that sent me. If any man will do his will, he shall know of the doctrine, whether it be of God, or whether I speak of myself. He that speaketh of himself seeketh his own glory: but he that seeketh his glory that sent him, the same is true, and no unrighteousness is in him.*
>
> *John 7:16–18*

Jesus was totally surrendered to the will of His Father. He did not pursue His personal ambition or desire. Instead, He spent time in prayer, seeking His Father's instructions.

And in the morning, rising up a great while before day, he went out,
and departed into a solitary place, and there prayed.

Mark 1:35

Revival churches press deeper in prayer and worship. They are not consumed with doing things in the flesh but by the Spirit.

Radical obedience brings radical blessings. Abraham was called by God to step out and leave everything comfortable and familiar (Genesis 12). Revival centers understand that obeying the voice of the Lord brings His glory. God wants to move in the gifts of the Holy Spirit with healing power, deliverance, and salvation. These moves of God only come through prayer and obedience.

Revival churches and ministries are delivered from what people think. As long as spiritual leaders bow to the controlling powers of men, they will never do great exploits. In order to move in revival you must be a God-pleaser not a man-pleaser.

Revival churches must:

Enter deeper realms of prophetic worship. There are songs birthed by the Spirit of God that will change the spiritual complexion of entire churches, cities, and regions. God is raising up a radical new generation of worshippers who will bring His glory to earth.

Have fiery preaching. The leaders of these ministries will be people who speak forth the fire and power of God.

Flow in life-changing miracles. Revival ministries value the anointing of God and create an atmosphere where miracles manifest every day.

Raise up prayer teams. Nothing leaves heaven and comes to earth without prayer. Every revival ministry must have teams of people who seek the face of God for their city.

Promote and establish ministry teams. The fire of revival will be brought forth by teams of people who have been joined together by the Spirit of God. Revival churches raise up and send forth ministry teams to help fulfill the vision.

These are just a few of the vital keys in revival ministries. There are many more things that God is showing His people about building a revival center. If you are a leader, embrace the call to buck the normal system of doing church. Step out by faith and dive deeper into the things of the Spirit. God is calling forth a new generation of ministers who will build places of the Spirit and not lean on the arm of the flesh.

If you are a believer looking for a place to connect, get to a revival center. Don't get trapped in the flow of religious ministry. God wants to introduce you to a deeper passion than you have ever known. This is a time marked by God for divine visitation. We are encountering God in miraculous ways that will change the generations.

Step out of ***normality*** and into the ***fire of revival!***

The Word of God is fuel for revival. As the power of the Holy Spirit meets the life-giving force of the Word of God, revelation comes forth. In the midst of revival, Teachers, Apostles and Pastors will bring forth messages that have been born of the Spirit during times of intense prayer. These messages lay the foundation for the move of the Spirit that will follow and set the captive free.

Whom they set before the apostles: and when they had prayed, they laid their hands on them. And the word of God increased; and the number of the disciples multiplied in Jerusalem greatly; and a great company of the priests were obedient to the faith. And Stephen, full of faith and power, did great wonders and miracles among the people.

Acts 6:6-8

In Jesus' ministry and in the ministry of the Early Church there was a combination of Word and power. The Word was boldly declared and the power of God confirmed the Word.

And Jesus went about all Galilee, teaching in their synagogues, and preaching the gospel of the kingdom, and healing all manner of sickness and all manner of disease among the people. And his fame went throughout all Syria: and they brought unto him all sick people that were taken with divers diseases and torments, and those which were possessed with devils, and those which were lunatick, and those that had the palsy; and he healed them.

Matthew 4:23-24

It is often easy for preachers in this generation to recycle information believing that the more information that they share the more victory and power the Church will walk in. The great deception in that thinking is that information alone does not produce power or lasting change. It is only when the information becomes revelation that faith is unlocked and supernatural victory comes. Let's examine the most fundamental concept of faith for a moment.

So then faith cometh by hearing, and hearing by the word of God.

Romans 10:17

For many years I believed that faith was the result of information, that the more teaching, reading, and studying I did the more my faith would grow. Then one day in prayer, the Holy Spirit took me to the verse above (Romans 10:17) and told me to look up the word "*word*" in that verse. When I checked to see what "*word*" was in the original text, I found it was the Greek word *rhema* which means "spoken word" not *logos* which means "written word." Why is this important? It is a key to understanding the operation of faith because a *rhema* word is a revealed word. It is something that God speaks, breathes upon, and illuminates to you. The building of faith is the direct result of prayer, meditation (pondering the word), and Spirit-led study. The Holy Ghost acts as your Teacher (John 14:26) and guides you into the truth (revealed word). When the Holy Spirit shows you something from the Word of God, your faith is then established in that area and the devil can no longer steal from you in that particular area.

One of the keys of revival is ministers who speak the messages that have been revealed to them in their private time with God. In those revealed words is contained both the faith and the power necessary to break bondages and set captives free.

He that hath an ear, let him hear what the Spirit saith unto the churches.

Revelations 2:7

Jesus, the Head of the Church, is longing to talk to His people. We must have men and women of God in this hour who will share messages from the Word of God that have been breathed upon by God as prophetic messages for this generation.

I have yet many things to say unto you, but ye cannot bear them now. Howbeit when he, the Spirit of truth, is come, he will guide you into all truth: for he shall not speak of himself; but whatsoever he shall hear, that shall he speak: and he will shew you things to come. He shall glorify me: for he shall receive of mine, and shall shew it unto you. All things that the Father hath are mine: therefore said I, that he shall take of mine, and shall shew it unto you.

John 16:12-15

The Holy Spirit has been sent to earth as our Prayer Partner, Helper, and Master Teacher. As we spend quality time with Him in prayer, He will reveal things from the Word of God that will establish our minds in truth and our spirits in faith. This is the type of preaching and ministry that feeds the embers of revival. As men and woman have been touched by God, they stand and declare the Word of the Lord to the Church. God's power comes to back up what they are saying because they are not just sharing their own thoughts, good principles, or messages they heard from someone else, they are sharing the life-giving Word of God Almighty.

The devil understands the power that is contained in the revealed Word of God. In fact, he is all too eager to see the Church embrace methods and movements that are not rooted in the Word but tantalize the flesh and tickle the ears. There have been many revival movements that ended in shipwreck because they were not rooted and grounded in the Word of God.

And when much people were gathered together, and were come to him out of every city, he spake by a parable: A sower went out to sow his seed: and as he sowed, some fell by the way side; and it was trodden down, and the fowls of the air devoured it. And some fell upon a rock; and as soon as it was sprung up, it withered away, because it lacked moisture. And some fell among thorns; and the thorns sprang up with it, and choked it. And other fell on good ground, and sprang up, and bare fruit an hundredfold. And when he had said these things, he cried, He that hath ears to hear, let him hear. And his disciples asked him, saying, What might this parable be? And he said, Unto you it is given to know the mysteries of the kingdom of God: but to others in parables; that seeing they might not see, and hearing they might not understand. Now the parable is this: The seed is the word of God. Those by the way side are they that hear; then cometh the devil, and taketh away the word out of their hearts, lest they should believe and be saved. They on the rock are they, which, when they hear, receive the word with joy; and these have no root, which for a while believe, and in time of temptation fall away. And that which fell among thorns are they, which, when they have heard, go forth, and are choked with cares and riches and pleasures of this life, and bring no fruit to perfection. But that on the good ground are they, which in an honest and good heart, having heard the word, keep it, and bring forth fruit with patience.

Luke 8:4–15

The battle in this parable is for the Word. The enemy is terrified of what can happen to an individual or a group of people when the Word of God becomes more than information to them but is revelation to them. When the Word becomes revelation, several things happen:

1. *It is no longer an abstract story or principle. It is truth to whom it has been revealed.*

2. *Faith arises and produces substance for hope.*

3. *Faith pleases God and ultimately receives from God.*

4. *Action accompanies the revelation of faith-*

> *But wilt thou know, O vain man, that faith without works is dead?*   *James 2:20*

The fowl of the air that are mentioned in the parable of the sower are actual demon spirits whose sole purpose is to rob God's people of revelation. Revelation fuels faith, faith unlocks power and power generates revival!

> *Let a man so account of us, as of the ministers of Christ, and stewards of the mysteries of God.*
>
>   *1 Corinthians 4:1*

Paul reveals a deep truth in this verse. An Apostle is a *sent one,* someone who has been divinely commissioned by God to impact a particular place or people group. One of the tools that God gives to an Apostle is revelation that has the power to transform the people to whom they are sent. Paul uses the word *stewards* here which means "manager". You can not manage something that you are not in charge of! God has placed revelation from His Word in the spirits of apostolic gifts in order to release unknown dimensions of Himself to the Body of Christ and to the world. In simple terms: these Apostles are sent with a word!

And lest I should be exalted above measure through the abundance of the revelations, there was given to me a thorn in the flesh, the messenger of Satan to buffet me, lest I should be exalted above measure.

2 Corinthians 12:7

Paul faced the same attack that we see demonstrated in the parable of the sower. A demon spirit that was sent as a *thorn in the flesh* attacking him on various fronts was sent because of the abundance of revelations. Satan understood that Paul had apprehended realms of God that would change the course of generations so he attacked him in order to stifle the revelation knowledge that he possessed. This revelation was not just information but life-giving mysteries that had been revealed as Paul spent time with the Holy Ghost. People have mistakenly thought that God was behind this thorn because He told Paul that the answer to the thorn was found in His grace. Why would God who gave the revelation to Paul then attempt to stop him from sharing the revelation? He would not and He did not! In fact, He desires all of His people to walk in revelation. He has sent the Holy Ghost to us to reveal the mysteries of God to our hearts, minds, and spirits and He has sent five ministry gifts (Apostles, Prophets, Evangelists, Pastors, and Teachers) to the Church as an act of His grace to reveal dimensions of His love to us. When God spoke to Paul about His grace, what He was revealing to Paul is that all authority had been given to him and that he could get rid of this demonic messenger by operating in the authority that was granted to him as a believer because of the grace of God. Like any believer who has gone through an extended battle, Paul had probably grown somewhat tired and went to the Lord in desperation. God reminded Paul that all power had been given to him and that he could turn the attacker away because of who he was in Christ!

Our fundamental belief systems in the Body of Christ are established by the teaching and doctrine that is declared to us. Many revival movements begin to entertain devils and fleshly operations because of the lack of solid teaching and doctrine. The enemy loves to put on a show in order to distract the saints from the deep cleansing, healing, and redemptive work of Christ. True revival must be one of Word and Spirit.

My brethren, be not many masters, knowing that we shall receive the greater condemnation. For in many things we offend all. If any man offend not in word, the same is a perfect man, and able also to bridle the whole body. Behold, we put bits in the horses' mouths, that they may obey us; and we turn about their whole body. Behold also the ships, which though they be so great, and are driven of fierce winds, yet are they turned about with a very small helm, whithersoever the governor listeth. Even so the tongue is a little member, and boasteth great things. Behold, how great a matter a little fire kindleth! And the tongue is a fire, a world of iniquity: so is the tongue among our members, that it defileth the whole body, and setteth on fire the course of nature; and it is set on fire of hell.

James 3:1-6

The word *masters* in the above verse is a Greek word that means "teachers". In this parable we see the power that the tongue has in our individual lives as believers. We can speak life or death, blessing or cursing but there is an even deeper message that is often overlooked. The office of a Teacher is being revealed in this parable and the powerful effects that the teaching ministry has upon the Body of Christ. This one small member can guide the entire body into truth that brings life and freedom or deception that brings death and bondage.

The Body of Christ will follow the direction that is established by the teaching that is set before them. If they are receiving true doctrine then they will advance forward in the mighty things of God. If they are receiving false doctrine then they will be bound and not enjoy all that God has for them.

> *For as he thinketh in his heart, so is he: Eat and drink, saith he to thee; but his heart is not with thee.*
>
> *Proverbs 23:7*

The thoughts (beliefs, self-image, understanding of God) that are locked deep inside our heart will guide our lives. Many times through the years I have ministered to someone who had seen a truth in the Word of God and desired to enjoy that truth but had great difficulty receiving because of things they were taught years earlier.

The teaching ministry lays very deep foundations in the lives of people which brings guidance to their lives. It is very uncommon for me to allow a negative thought to dominate my thinking and limit my faith. This is because I have been taught for many years that I can cast down any thought that is contrary to the Word of God and break the strongholds in my mind. My life is following the direction that has been established deep in my inner man through teaching, prayer, meditation of the Word, and personal revelation.

We must contend for truth in the Body of Christ. Paul as an Apostle, guarded the churches that he had influence over and warned them about false teaching because he understood the power that fundamental belief systems hold.

> *This charge I commit unto thee, son Timothy, according to the prophecies which went before on thee, that thou by them mightest war a good warfare; Holding faith, and a good conscience; which some having put away concerning faith have made shipwreck: Of whom is Hymenaeus and Alexander; whom I have delivered unto Satan, that they may learn not to blaspheme.*
>
> *1 Timothy 1:18-20*

> *I marvel that ye are so soon removed from him that called you into the grace of Christ unto another gospel: Which is not another; but there be some that trouble you, and would pervert the gospel of Christ.*
>
> *Galatians 1:6-7*

In both of these examples, Paul is talking to his spiritual children and advising them not to get involved in the particular teaching ministries that will produce deception. We must have truth and doctrinal clarity at the forefront of the move of God for this generation. It is gospel truth that will launch us into greater realms of power, mercy, and love.

> *Now the Spirit speaketh expressly, that in the latter times some shall depart from the faith, giving heed to seducing spirits, and doctrines of devils.*
>
> *1 Timothy 4:1*

This verse uncovers two opponents of true revival. The devil uses seducing spirits to draw men and women away from truth and into error. He uses doctrines of devils to establish wrong belief systems and thus changes the course of living for those affected.

There have been many movements within the Body of Christ that ended in disaster because of the operations of these wicked spiritual forces. In these last days, it is not good enough to just see manifestations of the supernatural, we must make sure that what we are doing is rooted in truth.

In a recent time of prayer, the Spirit of the Lord came to me real strong and began to warn me about the operation of doctrines of devils in these closing moments of the Church age. He told me that there would be many things that man would label as revival which would ultimately be revealed as false operations fueled by demonic demonstration. He also showed me ministers who once preached and stood boldly on truth who would begin to buy into a lie and spread that lie with tenacity. I asked the Lord how these things could be. Why do good gospel preachers suddenly seem overtaken with false doctrine? He began to reveal to me the operations of these spirits.

The first thing that the devil does when he wants to pollute the Body of Christ with a false doctrine is to search for a minister over whom he can gain influence. This is most likely someone who has been having some type of inward struggle that few people know about. That struggle could be an unexplained tragedy, a moral battle, or a just pressure from the cares of life. When the devil identifies an area of weakness, he then sends a tormenting spirit to the mind of that minister. That spirit begins to bring up a multitude of questions. The tormenting spirit asks the mind of the minister why certain things happen, why calamity comes, why there is suffering in the world, why particular lifestyles are declared unlawful by scripture, why we are despised by the world, and many other questions that are difficult for the mind of the minister.

The devil has been watching the minister waiting for an opportune time. He looses the tormenting spirit at a point when the minister has dropped his shield of faith.

Finally, my brethren, be strong in the Lord, and in the power of his might. Put on the whole armour of God, that ye may be able to stand against the wiles of the devil. For we wrestle not against flesh and blood, but against principalities, against powers, against the rulers of the darkness of this world, against spiritual wickedness in high places. Wherefore take unto you the whole armour of God, that ye may be able to withstand in the evil day, and having done all, to stand. Stand therefore, having your loins girt about with truth, and having on the breastplate of righteousness; And your feet shod with the preparation of the gospel of peace; Above all, taking the shield of faith, wherewith ye shall be able to quench all the fiery darts of the wicked. And take the helmet of salvation, and the sword of the Spirit, which is the word of God: Praying always with all prayer and supplication in the Spirit, and watching thereunto with all perseverance and supplication for all saints.

Ephesians 6:10-18

Our armor is the key to victory! We must be covered in the full armor of God which comes through prayer and spending time in the Word. The Bible says that above all we are to take the covering of the shield of faith. The Lord told me one time that many people go through seasons in which they back off in prayer and drop their shield. It is in those seasons that they become extremely vulnerable to the works of the enemy, in particular discouragement, offense, and strife. The believer could go through the exact same situation one week before with their shield of faith covering their heart and not be influenced by the enemy but now that they have dropped their shield, the enemy is able to touch their heart.

Torment is released during a season when the minister has not been covering themselves with their shield of faith. Torment comes with negative thoughts, painful lies, and difficult questions.

The key here is that we cannot allow our minds to wander and meditate (ponder) on negative questions. There are things that happen in the earth that we are not able to understand without the manifest wisdom of God. We must take those things and give them over to the Lord in prayer. When we feel ourselves getting discouraged, we must dig into the Word and prayer. If a believer or minister allows himself to question the Word and meditate on negative things without prayer, they open the door for the devil to come in with deception. It is okay to go to God with questions but you must stay in the Word, stay in prayer, and determine to trust God.

Things will happen in the natural realm that we as humans do not understand. We must hold fast to the Word of God. We can not let our experiences on earth override our faith in the eternal Word of God. Jesus does not stop being a saviour because someone we know refuses salvation. He does not stop being a healer because someone we know dies early. The Word is truth and it never changes! The Word of God is the final authority in the life of a believer and in ministry.

In the beginning was the Word, and the Word was with God, and the Word was God.

John 1:1

Another key to keeping your faith strong in moments of questioning is to pray in other tongues.

But ye, beloved, building up yourselves on your most holy faith, praying in the Holy Ghost. Praying in the Holy Ghost builds you up.

Jude 20

Praying in the Holy Ghost ministers peace to you:

For with stammering lips and another tongue will he speak to this people. To whom he said, This is the rest wherewith ye may cause the weary to rest; and this is the refreshing: yet they would not hear.

Isaiah 28:11

Praying in the Holy Ghost unlocks mysteries and releases the Master Teacher:

For he that speaketh in an unknown tongue speaketh not unto men, but unto God: for no man understandeth him ; howbeit in the spirit he speaketh mysteries.

1 Corinthians 14:2

After the devil has filled the mind of the targeted minister with doubt and fear, he has weakened their faith. They have dropped their shield and are not spending quality time praying and meditating the Word. Now the tormenting spirit partners with a familiar spirit that mimics the presence of God and enters into their life withdrawing all the feelings of torment for a moment. Because this minister has been under almost constant

attack, they are shocked at the peace they feel when the tormenting spirit lifts its torment for a moment. Then the familiar spirit
convinces the minister that the feelings of peace are actually the
presence of God. As the minister is experiencing these things, the
devil then introduces them to a demonic doctrine and convinces
the minister that it is, in fact, truth. The minister takes the bait and
believes that they have had an encounter with God because of all
the soulish feelings that they have experienced on the heels of a
severe attack. What they fail to realize is that they have not heard
from God but have been deceived by a familiar spirit.

The minister will come away from this experience convinced
that they have a new revelation that will change the world. In
some ways that is true but the change will not be for good! They
are now a tool in the devil's bag of tricks to keep the Body of
Christ from real power and authority which is the fruit of truth.

As the minister begins to proclaim the doctrine of devils
that has been given to them, familiar spirits will work with them,
through lying signs and wonders. False manifestations will con-
vince those who are not rooted in the truth that what is taking
place is a move of God.

> *When Pharaoh shall speak unto you, saying, Shew a miracle for*
> *you: then thou shalt say unto Aaron, Take thy rod, and cast it before*
> *Pharaoh, and it shall become a serpent. And Moses and Aaron went*
> *in unto Pharaoh, and they did so as the Lord had commanded: and*
> *Aaron cast down his rod before Pharaoh, and before his servants, and*
> *it became a serpent. Then Pharaoh also called the wise men and the*
> *sorcerers: now the magicians of Egypt, they also did in like manner*

with their enchantments. For they cast down every man his rod, and they became serpents: but Aaron's rod swallowed up their rods.

Exodus 7:9-12

As the power of God was at work through Aaron, the power of the enemy was at work through Pharoah's sorcerers and magicians. The devil mimicked what God was doing. That is how familiar spirits operate, they imitate the presence of God to draw people away from God.

The ultimate goal of the devil is to lead people away from basic Bible doctrine, destroy faith, and wreck the Word of God.

Conclusion

Revival is marked by a flow of the supernatural power of God. When God visits a church, territory, or region with revival there are supernatural signs and wonders. Many people in today's generation have not encountered the power of God. The Church has drifted off course, abandoning its foundations for man's plans, concepts, and strategies.

In the absence of the supernatural power of God, other spiritual forces will rise up and attempt to fill the void. The devil sends demonic messengers to seduce society and draw people away from God's Holy presence.

There shall not be found among you any one that maketh his son or his daughter to pass through the fire, or that useth divination, or an observer of times, or an enchanter, or a witch, Or a charmer, or a consulter with familiar spirits, or a wizard, or a necromancer. For all

*that do these things are an abomination unto the Lord: and because
of these abominations the Lord thy God doth drive them out from
before thee.*

Deuteronomy 18:1-12

Any spiritual practice that is not rooted in the Word and powered by the Holy Ghost is strictly forbidden. We are living in a time when the world is hungry for the supernatural. They are walking around with a God-sized hole in their being, longing to be filled. The world draws them away with occultic practices and new age philosophies while denying the true power of Jesus Christ. The anti-Christ spirit has invaded society and made the mention of the name of Jesus offensive in many realms.

Much of the Church has drifted drastically off course, moving away from gospel foundations. They build their services around self-help talks and powerless music. People flock to these churches every weekend looking to fill the void, but leave empty because there is no power.

This set of circumstances has created an atmosphere that makes it easy for deception to affect the people of God.

*And Nadab and Abihu, the sons of Aaron, took either of them his
censer, and put fire therein, and put incense thereon, and offered
strange fire before the   Lord, which he commanded them not. And
there went out fire from the Lord, and devoured them, and they
died before the Lord.*

Leviticus 10:1-2

Aaron's sons were charged with priestly duties. As they did what they believed was right, it ministered death instead of life. What happened? They offered a strange fire! God's fire is holy (separate), pure and consuming. These two priests offered a fire that did not please God, instead they kindled the anger of the Lord.

This same thing occurs in today's Church world. There are times when false manifestations and strange fires invade Christian culture and come to seduce the people of God. These strange fires are sent to draw people away from strong foundations.

This example teaches us that there can be spiritual manifestations that come forth and demonstrate a certain realm of power, yet it is not from the Lord. The end-time Church must be a discerning church!

Three keys to discern strange fire:

1.) Examine the fruit of the ministry. Does their ministry have a proven record? Are they balanced in the Word? Are their lives in order?

> *Beware of false prophets, which come to you in sheep's clothing, but inwardly they are ravening wolves.16 Ye shall know them by their fruits. Do men gather grapes of thorns, or figs of thistles?*
>
> *Matthew 7:15-16*

2.) Be prayed up and follow your inner witness. Questioning a spiritual manifestation is not a sin! If something in your spirit man does not bear witness with a spiritual manifestation then don't get involved with it. This is Holy Ghost protection.

Beloved, believe not every spirit, but try the spirits whether they are of God: because many false prophets are gone out into the world.

1 John 4:1

3.) Does the manifestation line up with the Word? If a ministry is saying or doing things that are not found in the Word of God then they are wrong and should be rebuked.

In the beginning was the Word, and the Word was with God, and the Word was God

John 1:1

We do not have to live in fear of strange fire. We have the Holy Ghost living in us. He will lead us and guide us into all truth! God's people are hungry for moves of His Spirit and those moves are coming forth in this hour through pure vessels. We must, however, be aware that the stronger the Holy Ghost works the more the enemy will try to rise up right in the midst of that working and bring forth deception.

We do not need more false moves or misguided ministers to pollute the move of God and disappoint the Body of Christ. We are longing for a demonstration of the *Holy Fire of God.*

A divination generation-

And it came to pass, as we went to prayer, a certain damsel possessed with a spirit of divination met us, which brought her masters much gain by soothsaying: The same followed Paul and us, and cried, saying, These men are the servants of the most high God, which shew unto us the way of salvation.18 And this did she many days. But

Paul, being grieved, turned and said to the spirit, I command thee
in the name of Jesus Christ to come out of her. And he came out the
same hour.

Acts 16:16-18

God visited Paul and sent him on an apostolic mission to
bring the gospel in power and might to a region. As he is
ministering, he is met by this young lady who is possessed
with a spirit of divination. The spirit of divination is a py-
thon spirit that comes to choke the life, breath, and wind
of God out of the Church. This spirit is also a fortune-
telling spirit. This young lady made a lot of money for her
masters by telling people their fortunes.

Quench not the Spirit. Despise not prophesyings.

1 Thessalonians 5:19-20

The Church should be speaking to the world under the inspiration of the Holy Ghost. We have been given a prophetic
anointing to declare the will of God over the lives of people. The
direction that hungry people seek is found in the midst of the
presence of God. Yet, much of the Church has kicked the gift of
prophecy out the door. When hungry people come in, all they get
is a canned message that is void of power and demonstration.

This young woman mentioned in Acts chapter sixteen was
telling people about their future by operating in the power of a
demon spirit. She was so successful because prior to Paul's arrival
there were no servants of God who were filled with the Word of
the Lord with demonstration.

She followed Paul around saying things that sounded right. Strange fire will sound right and may even look right, yet it is not right. It is rooted in spirits that are not the Spirit of God. This girl did not say or do anything that was outwardly wrong, yet Paul became grieved deep in his spirit man and confronted the devil that was operating through her.

As we move into a greater time of outpouring, apostolic and prophetic voices will arise and bring a cleansing to the Body of Christ. We have had too much strange fire in the House of the Lord and few leaders have had the courage to confront it because of the fear of man.

When Paul confronted this spirit, the whole city got angry. They could not see what Paul saw because they were not walking in the realm of the Spirit like Paul was. This is often the case in the Church today when strange fire is in operation. Many people are drawn to the fire but it is the devil's light show. They want to see what is happening, they are hungry for something more. Yet, the foundation is not rooted and grounded in the Word and the spiritual power is not holy. When leaders rise up and declare the operation of the strange fire to be unlawful, members of the Body and weak leaders get angry and turn against the very voices that God is using to protect them.

> *Regard not them that have familiar spirits, neither seek after wizards, to be defiled by them: I am the Lord your God.*
>
> *Leviticus 19:31*

What is a familiar spirit? It is a mimicking spirit. The Bible talks about this spirit pretending to be a dead person. This spirit imitates people and can imitate the very presence of God.

The devil knows that most Christians would never willingly turn toward him to embrace sin and bondage. He comes in with very subtle deception. He brings forth false operations in order to draw the people of God off the path that the Lord has placed them on and to distract them. This is the assignment of a familiar spirit.

We are living in a time when the Church and the nations need the holy power of God. True revival involves a partnership of the Word and the Spirit working together to break bondages. We do not need to be afraid of strange fire but simply aware of its attempt to come against the true work of revival.

The Fire of Revival

I know that the Lord visited me with the teaching contained in this book. While writing these words, the Spirit of the Lord has overwhelmed me with His desire to move in the midst of His people. I truly believe that we are living in a time when God wants to do great and glorious things in the lives of His beloved.

I pray that you hear what the Spirit of the Lord is saying in this hour. May this writing serve as a call to an awakening in the Body of Christ. Jesus, the Head of the Church, is calling His Bride to awaken to His glory. In these moments of revival, a holy hunger is being released inside the children of God. The purpose of this hunger is to provide what is needed for the believer to reach out in the spirit and take hold of the power needed to change.

The coming days will be both exciting and challenging. These are the days when the Kingdom of God is coming forth in full effect. Men and women who have been alone with God will come to the forefront with divine revelation and authority. They will refuse to buy into the powerless religious systems that have held the glory of God back. These revivalists are ablaze with the pure fire of revival. You have a place in this moment! No matter what your gifting or calling is, Jesus is asking you to yield fully to Him. As you lay your life down in order to embrace a journey of surrender and full commitment, you will find Jesus in all of His glory.

I pray for you that the fire of God is completely turned loose in your spirit, that from this day forward you enter into another level of your walk with God. You will not be ordinary, but extraordinary. God's Kingdom is released in every part of your life in Jesus' name. You shall do great and mighty things for God. You will move in sync with His voice with no confusion or stumbling. The Father will release His love and grace in every area of your life.

Go forward marked with the spirit of awakening and burn with *The Fire of Revival!*

PRAYER OF SALVATION

God loves you—no matter who you are, no matter what
your past. God loves you so much that He gave His one and only
begotten Son for you. The Bible tells us that "...whoever
believes in him shall not perish but have eternal life" (John 3:16
NIV). Jesus laid down His life and rose again so that we could
spend eternity with Him in heaven and experience His absolute
best on earth. If you would like to receive Jesus into your life,
say the following prayer out loud and mean it from your heart.

*Heavenly Father, I come to You admitting that I am
a sinner. Right now, I choose to turn away from sin, and
I ask You to cleanse me of all unrighteousness. I believe
that Your Son, Jesus, died on the cross to take away my
sins. I also believe that He rose again from the dead so
that I might be forgiven of my sins and made righteous
through faith in Him. I call upon the name of Jesus
Christ to be the Savior and Lord of my life. Jesus, I
choose to follow You and ask that You fill me with the
power of the Holy Spirit. I declare that right now I am
a child of God. I am free from sin and full of the righteousness of God. I am saved in Jesus' name. Amen.*

If you prayed this prayer to receive Jesus Christ as your
Savior for the first time, please contact us on the Web at
www.harrisonhouse.com to receive a free book.

Or you may write to us at

Harrison House • P.O. Box 35035 • Tulsa, Oklahoma 74153

Fast. Easy.
Convenient.

For the latest Harrison House product information and author news, look no further than your computer. All the details on our powerful, life-changing products are just a click away. New releases, E-mail subscriptions, testimonies, monthly specials—find it all in one place. Visit harrisonhouse.com today!

harrisonhouse

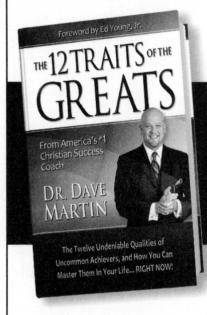